History of the Independent Loudoun Virginia Rangers. U.S. vol. cav. (scouts) 1862-65

ALL QUIET ON THE POTOMAC.

HISTORY

OF THE

INDEPENDENT LOUDOUN VIRGINIA RANGERS.

U. S. VOL. CAV.
(SCOUTS)

1862-65.

BY BRISCOE GOODHART,
CO A.

WASHINGTON, D. C.
PRESS OF MCGILL & WALLACE
1896.

PREFACE

As the basis of every great national achievement is to be found in the thoughts and feelings of the people, so the real history of a great army is founded upon the annals of the separate organizations of which it was composed.

The " History of the Loudoun (Virginia) Rangers," as feebly set forth in the following pages, claims attention as a part, however small, in the history of one of the greatest wars the world has ever known.

As the name of their organization indicates, they came from a State which was arrayed in arms against the authority of the National Government. No Governor, or Senator, or Member of Congress guarded their interests, nor was any State or local bounty held forth to them as an allurement. Their enlistment in the Union Army—their country's army—was the spontaneous outgrowth of a spirit of lofty patriotism.

As they saw their duty they were not lacking in moral courage to perform that duty ; and with no lapse of years shall we ever fail to insist that the principles for which the Rangers contended were eternally right, and that their opponents were eternally wrong.

While most of the events narrated in this work passed under the personal observation of the writer, he has also made use of reliable information from every available source.

He desires to express his grateful sense of obligation to those who have materially lessened his labors and largely contributed to the value of his work by furnishing useful materials, such as reports, letters, diaries, etc.

Should these pages interest the reader the writer will feel that his labors have not been in vain.   B G.

WASHINGTON, D C., 1896.

CONTENTS.

CHAPTER I.

CHAPTER II.

CHAPTER III

CHAPTER IV.

CHAPTER V

CHAPTER VI.

CHAPTER VII.

HISTORY

OF THE

LOUDOUN (VA.) RANGERS.

CHAPTER I

EARLY FORMATION OF LOUDOUN COUNTY—EARLY EMIGRANTS—CAVALIER·—
GERMANS—QUAKERS—GENISIS OF THE RANGERS

President Lincoln's call for 300,000 troops in the summer of 1862 touched a responsive chord in the hearts of nearly 600,000 patriots. Into this vast aggregation of volunteer soldiers the Loudoun (Virginia) Rangers cast their little mite. Possibly the Rebellion could have been suppressed without them, yet that Grand Army that marched to the music of the Union, from Fort Sumter to Appomattox, was composed of just such mites. The command was recruited in Loudoun County, Virginia, and mustered into the United States service at Lovettsville, the 20th day of June, 1862. It was an independent command, organized in obedience to a special order of the Honorable Edwin M. Stanton, Secretary of War, and was at first subject to his orders only, but subsequently merged into the Eighth Corps, commanded at that time by the venerable Major General John Ellis Wool, hero of three wars—the second war with Great Britain in 1812, the Mexican War, 1847, and the Civil War, 1861–'65—an honor that has been enjoyed by comparatively few

Perhaps the reader may inquire how the Rangers came to be arrayed on the side of the Union, coming as they did from within the territory of the alleged Southern Confederacy. The answer is, "Blood will tell." A majority of the citizens of Loudoun County cast their wavering fortunes under the seductive folds of the Stars and Bars, and fought with a courage and a desperation worthy of a better cause. They, like thousands of other so-called "loyal sons of the South," were carried away by the plausible delusion of "States' Rights," to fight against the Government in which they lived, and which afforded them protection But while a majority of the citizens of Loudoun County was extreme Secessionist, a determined and enthusiastic minority was just as firm in its loyalty to the flag of its country as was any section of the Union

Owing to the meagreness of colonial history it is impossible to state the exact period this section of the State was settled. The first record we have of an attempt at settlement is in 1670, when Capt. Henry Batte organized an expedition from the head of tidewater on the Potomac (probably near Alexandria), passing up that stream and crossing the Blue Ridge at or near Snicker's Gap, invading the Shenandoah Valley. The Indians did not look with favor upon this intrusion of their territory, as a war of extermination against the few settlers was waged with great fury for the next five years, terminating in a great battle on the site of the City of Washington, resulting in a defeat of the red skins

In 1700 Gov. Sir William Berkeley assumed a very friendly attitude towards the Indians, gradually extending settlements on the western frontier. In 1716 Gov. Spotswood visited this section, and the visit is known in history as the "March of Spotswood." In a list of his equipage is to be found eight kinds of wine. On the summit of the Blue Ridge his party held a kind of banquet, or "passover," with the Indians

The desire among the early settlers to possess choice pieces of real estate developed slowly, consequently little progress was made in settling the country, yet intercourse with the savages had been kept up, resulting in a better acquaintance, which gradually led to a partial yielding on their part to the inevitable—the onward march of civilization.

Permanent settlements began about 1725. What is now Loudoun County was then a part of Prince William County, and owned by one man, Lord Thomas Fairfax, Baron of Cameron. The County was divided in 1742, and Fairfax County created and named in honor of the landlord, and in 1757 Fairfax County was divided and Loudoun County created and named in honor of Lord Loudoun, a prominent officer in the English Army, afterwards Commander in Chief of the British forces in the American Colonies, and Governor of Virginia from 1758–1762.

About the earliest settlers we have any authentic record of (1725) were the English Cavalier stock, who located in the eastern and southern portions of the county, extending from the Potomac River south to Middleburg and from the Catoctin and Bull Run Mountains east to the eastern border of the county This stock was the first to introduce and foster slavery in the county.

From 1725 to 1735, there came from Pennsylvania a sturdy and vigorous people who settled what is known as the German Settlement, extending west from the Catoctin Mountains to the Short Hill Mountains, and from the Potomac River south to near Wheatland. In 1710 to 1720 this same people had come from the Palatine States of Germany, and settled in New York and Pennsylvania.

The earliest date the Germans settled in Loudoun County is not exactly known History places the period at from 1725 to 1735. There is some evidence, however, that they came at an earlier date. The black-heart cherry tree that has flourished for centuries in Germany has been grown in this German settlement to perfection, and the growths of the oldest trees show it to have been planted in 1720. This is presuming, of course, that the seed was brought from Germany by these people.

There came about the same time members of the Society of Friends (Quakers) from England and from Ireland and settled in the central portions of the county, extending from Waterford south to Goose Creek.

The term Quaker, originally given in reproach, has been so often used by friend as well as foe, that it is no longer a term of derision, but is the generally accepted designation of a member of the Society of Friends. With this apology we shall use the word Quaker whenever we may have occasion to refer to them in the course of this narrative.

Both the Germans and Quakers left friends and all those pleasant associations that cluster around the place of nativity, and willingly assumed the dangers of a long and tedious voyage across the Atlantic, for the sake of liberty. When the French crossed the Rhine into Germany and waged a bitter war of persecution against those that dared to free themselves from the Romish hierarchy, thousands of Germans, the adherents of Luther, sought refuge in America, where they could worship God as their consciences dictated, with none to molest them or make them afraid.

The Quakers were also the victims of a similar persecution in England on account of their religion. Many of this people were cast into prison because they insisted on their own simple form of worship, "The Fatherhood of God and the Brotherhood of Men," and, because this was denied them, turned their faces to America, where liberty of both mind and body was guaranteed to all

Mr. Asa Moore (great grandfather of Mrs. Samuel C. Means) was one of the earliest emigrants of this people, one of the founders of Waterford, and he named it after his native town in Ireland. He built the first house in Waterford, which is still standing, and adjoins the residence of the late Capt. S. C. Means.

The Quakers also laid out the village of Hamilton, which they named Harmony.

The descendants of these people to a large extent still occupy the land settled by their ancestors. That portion of the country settled by the Germans and Friends, while it is no better, and perhaps not so highly favored as other sections, shows a higher development than any other section of the county. The well-tilled farms, the comfortable, though unpretentious houses, fine orchards, and all that pertains to a prosperous and happy people, are particularly noticeable. The indefatigable industry of this people is especially commendable, as everybody works at something, and there is absolutely not a pauper amongst them.

This territory of about 125 square miles contains more churches, school houses, mills and factories than can be found in the same number of square miles elsewhere in the County, and as a natural consequence the standard of intelligence and morality is exceptionally high.

It is no disparagement to the thousands of others that came to this country to state that the Germans came better fitted to battle against the inconveniences of a new country. To use a modern expression, "They came to stay" It is a remarkable coincidence that those that settled in Loudoun County represented every branch of industry.

To ascribe the many good qualities these early

settlers possessed entirely to the men would be a great injustice to the fair sex. While the men ploughed and planted, the women wove and spun. The first sheep in the county were brought from Germany by these people, and from the fleece of these the nimble fingers of the housewife fashioned clothing for the family, dyed by the barks and herbs of the forest into a diversity of colors, from which, by the ingenuity of the weaver, some gorgeous patterns were produced. Many specimens of their handiwork may be found amongst the early households. One of the most conspicuous, as well as the most useful of these, is the counterpane, or coverlet, of which we venture the assertion that no other section has produced this article in a more durable and artistic design than is here made. Many of them have been in use from fifty to one hundred years. Flax was also extensively raised, from which threads and summer fabrics were made for the household.

These people were pre-eminently Americans by adoption, if not by birth.

When the American colonies were threatened with subjugation the Germans did not hesitate to take up arms for their adopted country. Nearly every family had a representative in Washington's army.

It is a well-known fact that Loudoun County was one of the most densely populated counties in the State at that period, and at the close of the Revolution the county's militia numbered 1,750 men.

The county furnished the fifth President of the United States, in the person of James Monroe, the father of the famous Monroe Doctrine. It was here his neighbors and fellow-citizens gave him his political send-off in life, by electing him to the modest office of justice of the peace, which modest beginning finally led to the White House.

The census returns for fifty years previous to the war

of 1861 place Loudoun County in the first rank in improved farms, live-stock, wheat, corn, and fruits; the county contains valuable minerals, such as gold, iron, copper, salt, and marble. Some fine varieties of Loudoun marble were used in the construction of the Capitol at Washington. Those large columns in the old House and Senate chambers, of dark conglomerate marble, were taken from a Loudoun quarry.

The county can also boast of an honor that has been enjoyed by but few counties in the United States, as it contained the Capital of the United States for a brief period.

During our second war with Great Britain, the British had captured Washington August 24, 1814, and laid some of the public buildings in ruins, including the White House, or rather the red house as it was at that time. President Madison and his Cabinet loaded the archives of the Government into four four-horse wagons and hauled them to Leesburg, originally called George-town, where they exercised the functions of government for several weeks. The Declaration of Independence was among the valuables thus hauled away and saved.

The conservative citizens of Leesburg were not enthusiastic over so much prominence being thrust upon their quiet village, as they were probably fearful of the consequence, should the British come thus far

The President's wife was a Quakeress and a native of this section—the popular Dolly Madison

The first settlers, known as the Cavaliers, were firm advocates of slavery, and the inaugurators of State rights, and as a natural result their progeny grew up to espouse the cause of secession—in fact, they were "last ditchers."

While neither the Quakers nor the Germans favored slavery, their interpretation of State rights was uncompromising allegiance to the Union of States and the flag of their country, purchased and made sacred by the blood of their Revolutionary sires, and, as a sequence, their descendants grew up to oppose secession with all their might and main. Out of the loins of this people grew the Loudoun Rangers

The question of States' Rights is the rock upon which so many misguided State crafts have stranded, and it is deemed important to state the position of the Rangers on this all-important subject in the beginning. They were believers in States' Rights to the fullest acceptation of the term. They believed each State a part and parcel of the National compact that found a fuller and more permanent recognition of the United States of America as the supreme and governing power of this country, and it was the "State's right," and duty of the individual citizen, to render unfaltering allegiance to that power. They even went farther than this—they believed that when a State insisted on the right to secede from the National Government it is the duty of the parent government to proceed with due solemnity and take the rebellious State across the right knee and administer a spanking that would bring the adventurous and misguided member back to a full recognition of the authority of the parent government.

Capt. Samuel C. Means, Lieut. Edwin R Gover, Quartermaster Charles F. Anderson, Orderly Sergeant James A. Cox, Commissary Sergeant Edward T White, Sergeants Flemon B Anderson, David E. B. Hough, T. W. Franklin, Henry C. and Isaac S. Hough, Edward Bond, Samuel, William, Joseph F., George W , and Robert W Hough, Fenton P. and Charles F Rinker, from in and around Waterford, were, more or less, of Quaker lineage.

Lieut. Luther W. Slater, Sergeants James H. Beatty and John P Hickman, George V. Kern, Samuel, Joseph,

Capt. S. C. MEANS, Co. A.

and Peter C. Fry, Jacob Cordell, Samuel E. Tritapoe, George C. Tritapoe, Jacob E Boryer, Charles and George W. Baker, Samuel J. and W. J. Cooper, George P., John M , and Presley A. Davis, Thomas, Charles, and Henry Dixon, Armistead Everhart, Briscoe Goodhart, Philip H. Heater, Mahlon H Best, Edward Jacobs, Joseph T. Ritchie, John Ambrose, Charles F. Moreland, Albert C. Mock, John Lenhart, George Swope, Charles Stout, Charles L. Spring, Charles H Snoots, William Shoemaker, John W., Charles W., and Richard Virts, Frank Mormon, James Stoneburner, Johnathan Myers, Jacob Long, coming from around Lovettsville and Taylortown, were of German ancestry.

While a very large majority of the command belonged to the German and Quaker stock, there was quite a sprinkling of other nationalities, principally Scotch-Irish, comprising Lieut. D. M Keyes, W S Keyes, Sergeants James H. Corbin, Milton S. and James W. Gregg, Joseph T Divine, Bugler John S. Densmore, Michael McMullen, J. C. McCutcheon, D. J., George H., and Robert S Harper, John W. Forsythe, Peter Miles, Charles McDade, George Welch, James W and Sylvester Shackelford, and Joseph T. Cantwell.

The Quakers, on account of their religious faith, were strictly opposed to war, but when brought to the threshold of their own home the flesh grew stronger than the spirit, and in the late war quite a number laid down their lives that the Nation might live.

In one of the early battles of the late war one of that faith found himself on the skirmish line, with the bloodthirsty enemy in front. He selected his man and raised his trusty Enfield With the remark, "Friend, it is unfortunate, but thee stands exactly where I am going to shoot," he pulled the trigger, and when the smoke cleared away the enemy had one less to draw rations.

General Jacob Brown, the "fighting Quaker" and

Christian soldier, was a brigadier general in the second war with Great Britain, later a major general, and finally Commander in Chief of the United States Army from 1821 until his death in 1828. The hero of Chippewa, Niagara, and Erie, he was related to the ancestry of the wife of Captain Means and to many Quakers of Loudoun.

CHAPTER II.

The Secession Movement—Public Sentiment Against It—A Convention Called—An Election Ordered—Methods Employed in Forcing Virginia out of the Union

In 1861 the citizens of Virginia as well as several other Southern States found themselves very much divided on the question of secession. An undoubted majority was opposed to the new doctrine and had so expressed themselves on various occasions. Governor John Letcher convened the legislature in extraordinary session January 7, 1861, for the especial purpose of determining what attitude the Old Dominion should take on that all-absorbing question.

That august body decided to call a State convention to meet in Richmond February 15, to take such action as would best represent the majority of the citizens of the Commonwealth The Convention was composed of 152 delegates chosen February 4, and as was anticipated a majority of the delegates were opposed to the ordinance of secession. The convention convened February 15, and elected the Hon John Janney, a citizen of Loudoun County, as president, who on taking the chair made a strong and vigorous speech in the defense of the Union of States. After debating the question for three weeks the convention, April 4, rejected the ordinance of secession by a vote of 89 to 45, lacking one vote of being two to one against the measure, which was a great disappointment to the ultra secessionists, who had determined on a policy of rule or ruin. A system of threats and bribery was now resorted to that would cause a blush on the callous cheek of Cæsar. Their leaders grew desperate in their frenzy to have Virginia arrayed on their side to assist in waging a cruel and unjustifiable war on the best government that ever existed.

The Hon. R. M T. Hunter and other rabid secession leaders visited the largest cities of the State and held mass meetings, packed for the purpose of forestalling public opinion and adopting stereotyped resolutions, to be sent to the convention then in session in Richmond, to encourage that body in passing the ordinance of secession. A meeting for this purpose was held in Leesburg and addressed by J. M. Kilgore and others. Jefferson Davis sent Alexander H. Stephens from Montgomery to Richmond to use his persuasive eloquence on the convention, and assist in whipping-in those that were inclined to be refractory. Roger A. Pryor and Edmund Ruffin were dispatched to Charleston to urge an attack on Fort Sumter, hoping that the shedding of blood would inflame the passion of the Southern people and that the excitement that would follow would force Virginia to be arrayed against the National Government; and it did. The announcement in Richmond of the attack on Fort Sumter was followed by the booming of cannon and the waving of Confederate banners, yelling and parading of streets; in fact, pandemonium reigned and ruled supreme

Roger A. Pryor rose to be a major general in the Confederate army. When taken prisoner, Jeff. Davis accused him of desertion and going into the Federal lines. Pryor denied the charge, resigned, and enlisted and served to the close of the war as a private soldier, and is now (1896), having joined the cohorts of Tammany, a prominent judge of New York City. Edmund Ruffin pulled the lanyard and fired the first shot at Fort Sumter. After General Lee surrendered, Ruffin committed suicide by blowing the top of his head off, saying he wanted to die because the Confederacy could not live

Richmond was in the hands of a mob and ready to do their bidding. Meanwhile the system of intimidation and bribery had its effect; ten of the union delegates, apprehensive of the dangers that were threatening them, left the city for their homes. April 17 the convention in secret session passed the ordinance of secession by a vote of 88 to 55 on condition that it should be submitted to the people for their approval or rejection, at an election to be held the 23d of May, 1861, for that purpose Alexander H. Stephens and other Southern leaders were prolific with opinions that the action of the convention was final; that the State had already seceded, and that it did not require the action of the people further. The convention, however, insisted that the people must approve or disapprove the action already taken, and the election should be held for that purpose. The Southern leaders fully determined to stultify the voice of the people by ordering 50,000 rebel troops into Virginia to assist the dear people in making up their minds how to vote , and as by these troops the United States Government property at Harper's Ferry had been seized and the immense navy yard at Norfolk had been destroyed, this canvass and election as conducted was a mockery of justice. Many Union people had been driven from the State, or prohibited from voting; a number of citizens of Loudoun County had sought refuge in Maryland ; those that remained and insisted on voting ran great risk of personal injury. There was some disturbance at the polls at Lovettsville and Lincoln. A gentleman living near Leesburg and voting the Union ticket against secession was treated to a bath in a mud hole. Several were thrown in the Potomac River for the same offense. This was practically the beginning of the war in Virginia, as the rebel troops took a prominent part in the canvass, practically prohibiting the opposition from making a canvass. The result of the election was an endorsement of the action of the State convention in passing the ordinance of secession, the vote standing, for secession 125,950, against secession, 20,373. At this time the State contained over one million and a half population, and if an honest and fair election had been held should have polled at least 300,000 votes, but there was cast less than half that number. In these piping times of peace much is heard of the monstrosity of troops at an election. Bayonets at the polls should be used sparingly, and only to secure an honest expression of the will of the people. In this case they were used to prevent an honest expression of the will of the people. In Waterford, Lovettsville, Hoysville, and Neersville a majority was given against secession. This election was Virginia's first Appomattox, and for the honorable name she held in the sisterhood of States proved to be a hundred-fold more disastrous than the last Appomattox, when her shattered armies lay bleeding at every pore.

A sample of Confederate election returns taken from the Confederate archives is presented:

HEADQUARTERS VIRGINIA FORCES,
Richmond, Va., May 30, 1861.
Col. F. H. SMITH, *Richmond, Va.:*

COLONEL · I submit below the information you ask for the council. It is, of course, not strictly correct, though I think it is not far out of the way. It is impossible to get returns from these volunteers:

Norfolk, no returns, 7,000 conjectured; Jamestown Island, no returns, fifteen companies, 1,050; Williams-

burg and Yorktown, no returns, 3,500, Gloucester Point,
no returns, 600; West Point, 250; Richmond, including
Ashland and the Confederate States troops. 5,500, Fredericksburg, including counties on the lower Rappahannock and Potomac Rivers, number not known, 2,700;
Manassas Gap, no returns, 6,000, Leesburg, no returns,
500; Harper's Ferry, excluding Maryland troops, not
known, and excluding Point of Rocks, 5,500, Grafton,
no returns, 1,000 conjectured; Kanawha Valley, no returns, 1,100, Abingdon no returns, 500 conjectured;
Lynchburg, no returns, 1,000 conjectured; besides a few
companies supposed to be at Staunton, Charlottesville,
&c.   Total, 36,200.

I am, sir, very respectfully, &c.,

R. S. GARNETT,
Adjutant-General.

General Garnett was killed at Gettysburg, and, of
course, his secret of counting election returns is lost to
posterity.

Whether any of the troops voted against the ordinance
of secession we do not positively know; but we do know
if they did it was not counted, as 36,200, the number of
State troops in the field at that time, are returned as
voting solidly for the ordinance of secession   It is
known, however, that in some of the troops that were
recruited in the Shenandoah Valley, there was a majority of some commands that vigorously opposed the
ordinance of secession before and after election.

This election began to bear fruit early.   In less than
twenty days the Union people of West Virginia, who
would not submit to such tyranny, met in convention
at Wheeling (June 13), and organized a separate State
government, resolutions were adopted denouncing
secession, and offering their services to President Lincoln, which were gladly accepted, and a new State
was created.   The rebel government now had complete
control of the Old Dominion, and proceeded immediately to slay the goose that laid the golden egg.

In order that the reader may have a clearer conception of the men and methods employed in forcing Virginia, as well as other Southern States, out of the Union, a few extracts from the proceedings of the secession convention, also several Confederate orders relating to this section, is inserted.

Extract from proceedings of the Advisory Council of the State of Virginia.

SUNDAY, *April* 21, 1861.

*   *   *   *   *   *   *

It being considered desirable to ascertain the condition of affairs and the state of public opinion in Maryland, the Governor is respectfully advised to appoint Col James M. Mason a Commissioner to proceed forthwith to that State, and to acquire and communicate to the Governor such information as he may obtain.

*   *   *   *   *   *   *

MONDAY, *April* 22, 1861.

*   *   *   *   *   *   *

A telegram from John S. Barbour, Jr., confidential agent of the Government at Alexandria, asking for arms for the Maryland troops to enable them to resist the passage of Northern troops to Washington, who are said to be now concentrating near Baltimore, was submitted to the Council by the Governor for advice Whereupon his excellency was respectfully advised to send the following telegram to Mr. Barbour ·

"Telegraph received. Maj. Gen. Kenton Harper, in command at Harper's Ferry, is hereby ordered to deliver to General Steuart, at Baltimore, one thousand of the arms recently taken at Harper's Ferry.

*   *   *   *   *   *   *

It was also advised that the following telegram be sent to the Governor of Tennessee:

"The condition of affairs in Maryland and Virginia makes it important that we should know how far we may rely upon the co operation of Tennessee to repel an invasion of our common rights. Please communicate fully and without reserve. Answer at once."

*   *   *   *   *   *   *

Ordered, That the Governor be respectfully advised to communicate to the Convention, in secret session, the purport of the telegram in reference to the loan of arms to General Steuart, commanding the Maryland troops ; and also the telegram advised to be forwarded to the Governor of Tennessee.

Advised unanimously that the following telegram be returned in answer to Governor Harris .

"Since telegram of 22d of April, Convention has formed provisional agreement with Confederate States, placing troops of Virginia under control and direction of President of Confederate States. Those from Tennessee should be subject to same rule, and at Lynchburg can be provided for as troops of Virginia by Colonel Langhorne. Advise him."

*   *   *   *   *   *   *

PETERSBURG, VA., *April* 20, 1861.
L. P. WALKER, Secretary War, C. S. A.

Colonel Owen, president of the Virginia and Tennessee Railroad, has just reached here from Baltimore by way of Norfolk. He witnessed the butchery of Baltimore citizens by the Massachusetts regiment yesterday. He states the city is in arms and all are Southern men now. He says bridges north of Baltimore been burned, and no more troops can come from the North unless they march, and in large bodies, as Maryland is rising. Lincoln is in a trap. He has not more than twelve hundred regulars in Washington and not more than three thousand volunteers. We have three thousand in Harper's Ferry. Our boys, numbering four hundred, went down to-day to Norfolk to join the companies there and your forces coming from Charleston. You know how many we want. As leader we want Davis. An hour now is worth years of common fighting. One dash and Lincoln is taken, the country saved, and the leader who does it will be immortalized.

H. D. BIRD

BAPTIST CHURCH, at Waterford.—The Rangers' First Battle Ground.

RICHMOND, *May* 1, 1861.
Hon. L. P. WALKER.

Arrangements have been made to call out, if necessary, 50,000 volunteers from Virginia, to be rendezvoused at Norfolk, Richmond, Fredericksburg, Alexandria, Harper's Ferry, Grafton, Kanawha, Parkersburg, and Moundsville. Convention has authorized a provisional army of 10,000. Our troops are poorly armed Tolerable supply of powder ; deficient in caps.

JNO. LETCHER.

RICHMOND, *May* 3, 1861

By the Governor of Virginia.

A PROCLAMATION.

The sovereignty of the Commonwealth of Virginia having been denied, her territorial rights assailed, her soil threatened with invasion by the authorities at Washington, and every artifice employed which could inflame the people of the Northern States and misrepresent our purposes and wishes, it becomes the solemn duty of every citizen of this State to prepare for the impending conflict. These misrepresentations have been carried to such extent that foreigners and naturalized citizens who but a few years ago were denounced by the North and deprived of essential rights have now been induced to enlist into regiments for the purpose of invading this State, which then vindicated those rights and effectually resisted encroachments which threatened their destruction Against such a policy and against a force which the Government at Washington, relying upon its numerical strength, is now rapidly concentrating, it becomes the State of Virginia to prepare proper safeguards. To this end and for these purposes, and with a determination to repel invasion, I, John Letcher, Governor of the Commonwealth of Virginia, by authority of the Convention, do hereby authorize the commanding general of the military forces of this State to call out and cause to be mustered into the service of Virginia, from time to time, as the public exigencies may require, such additional number of volunteers as he may deem necessary.

Given under my hand, as Governor, and under the seal of the Commonwealth, at Richmond, this third day of May, 1861, and in the eighty-fifth year of the Commonwealth.

JOHN LETCHER.

By the Governor
    GEORGE W MUNFORD,
        Secretary of the Commonwealth.

———

HEADQUARTERS VIRGINIA FORCES,
Richmond, Va., May 1, 1861.

Col. T J JACKSON,
    Commanding Harper's Ferry, Va

You are desired to urge the transfer of all the machinery, materials, &c., from Harper's Ferry, as fast as possible, and have it prepared in Winchester for removal to Strasburg, whence it will be ordered to a place of safety. The machinery ordered to this place must be forwarded with dispatch, as has already been directed. The remainder will await at Strasburg further orders. All the machinery of the rifle factory, and everything of value therein, will be also removed as rapidly as your means will permit. If the troops can be advantageously used in the removal of the machinery, they will be so employed It is thought probable that some attack may be made upon your position from Pennsylvania, and you will keep yourself as well informed as possible of any movements against you. Should it become necessary to the defense of your position, you will destroy the bridges across the Potomac You are particularly directed to keep your plans and operations secret, and endeavor to prevent their being published in the papers of the country.

I am, sir, &c.,
            R. E. LEE,
        Major General, Commanding.

HEADQUARTERS VIRGINIA FORCES,

Richmond, Va., June 10, 1861.

Col. EPPA HUNTON, *Commanding, Leesburg, Va.:*

COLONEL. Your letter of the 8th instant has been received, and it is hoped that you have accomplished the destruction of the bridges upon the Loudoun and Hampshire Railroad, and otherwise rendered the road unserviceable to the enemy. Unless any of the rolling stock can be transferred to the Orange or Manassas Railroad, it must be destroyed immediately. Should it not already be demolished, the gondola and flats must not be permitted to fall into the hands of the enemy.

It is necessary to destroy the navigation of the Chesapeake and Ohio Canal, to prevent its being used by the enemy, and you will take measures to do so effectually, by cutting the dams at Seneca and Edwards Ferry, and blowing up the Monocacy aqueduct.

Respectfully, your obedient servant,

R. E LEE,
General, Commanding.

The bridges referred to in Gen. Lee's order were Shepherdstown, Harper's Ferry, Berlin, and Point of Rocks, and were burned Sunday, June 9, 1861.

The election of May 23, on the approval or disapproval of the passage of the ordinance of secession by the convention had not been held, and of course the State was still in the Union, yet we see that the State had actually been turned over to the Confederate government, while her citizens were blindly deceived by being asked to vote on that very question. The State militia, which had been organized, drilled, and partly equipped two years previous, was now ordered into the field under a reorganization.

The 56th Virginia militia, commanded by Col. William Giddings, was called out, and about 60 per cent, of the regiment that lived east of the Catoctin Mountain responded.

The Goresville company, or rather the remnant of that company that did not go to Maryland, was ordered to Cheek's Ford to guard the river and keep the Yankees from crossing at that point. It seems the captain of the company, John Money, was absent, and Campbell Belt, the quartermaster, was put in command Quartermaster Belt was somewhat of an inventive genius, a kind of a Col Mulberry Sellers. If the Confederacy had given him the slightest encouragement, no doubt he would have invented a kind of an infernal machine that would have demolished the whole Yankee nation in a jiffy ; but war does not always recognize genius, as was doubtless the case in this instance.

Quartermaster Belt had ordered quite a number of the farmers' harrows and had them placed in the river at the ford, claiming that it would tangle up the Yankee army if they attempted to cross. The Yankee forces on the Maryland side soon learned of the harrow scheme, and ordered out two companies, raised the harrows, and knocked out the teeth and shipped them North, where they were sold at good price, as samples of rebel weapons of war

Less then half of the Waterford company obeyed the call to be mustered into the rebel service. The company at Lovettsville sent ten men, and but four men went from the Hoysville company Those that refused to array themselves under the rebel banner were Union men and courted the displeasure of the secessionists, and must be severly disciplined. A bitter war of ostracism and revenge was resorted to. Quite a number of Union men had been particularly demonstrative and had not hesitated to express themselves for the Union and its flag on every occasion. This class was threatened with punishment or arrest.

It will be remembered that a large portion of the citizens of Loudoun County were intensely loyal to the National Government. Many of them were willing to and some did suffer death rather than take up arms against the United States. They were generally comfortably situated, by industry and economy had accumulated a fair share of this world's goods, and in maintaining their unswerving loyalty to the Union necessarily indicated a self sacrifice on their part of their property.

From Union citizens, who preferred to leave the State and all that was near and dear to them rather than go into the rebel army, their property, excepting their lands, was generally taken by that army.

They left their families in Loudoun, and if ever found visiting them they would be arrested and cast into a Southern prison, where their chances of life were very poor.

In December, 1861, William Smith, Armistead Magaha, Emanuel Ruse, and Isaac C Slater had come from Maryland to visit their families, and on returning had got to the ferry opposite Berlin (now Brunswick), where they were arrested as spies, taken to Richmond and confined in Libby prison, where they almost starved to death Slater, who was young and delicate, was reduced almost beyond recognition, and was years after his release regaining his health and strength

In April, 1861, the galling yoke of secession was made still more oppressive to the Union citizens of Loudoun. The Loudoun Cavalry (Confederate) visited the farmers in the German and the Quaker settlements, taking teams for the Confederate army. From many farmers a team of four horses and a wagon were taken, but where farmers were found with less than that number, one or two horses, or even one horse would be taken, and a wagon from others; thus making a complete four-horse team from one or two small farmers This property was taken with the promise that it would be returned ; but this promise, like other promises of the Confederacy, was never fulfilled, neither did any of the citizens receive any compensation for the property thus taken. If a citizen was found that did not possess either horse or wagon, he was pressed into service as a driver There was probably not a citizen in the territory above referred to whose property was not taken, and taken at a time when the Confederacy had money to pay for supplies, if they had been actuated by honest motives.

The Confederate archives are dumb with reference to this property

We insert Gen Beauregard's famous proclamation, "Beauty and Booty," it will be remembered by many of Loudoun's citizens

HEADQUARTERS DEPARTMENT OF ALEXANDRIA,
Camp Pickens, June 5, 1861.

To the good People of the Counties of Loudoun, Fairfax, and Prince William ·

A reckless and unprincipled tyrant has invaded your soil Abraham Lincoln, regardless of all moral, legal, and constitutional restraints, has thrown his abolition hosts among you, who are murdering and imprisoning your citizens, confiscating and destroying your property, and committing other acts of violence and outrage too shocking and revolting to humanity to be enumerated. All rules of civilized warfare are abandoned, and they proclaim by their acts, if not on their banners, that their war-cry is "Beauty and booty." All that is dear to man, your honor, and that of your wives and daughters, your fortunes, and your lives, are involved in this momentous contest

In the name, therefore, of the constituted authorities of the Confederate States, in the sacred cause of constitutional liberty and self government, for which we are contending, in behalf of civilization and humanity itself, I, G. T. Beauregard, brigadier general of the

Confederate States, commanding at Camp Pickens, Manassas Junction, do make this my proclamation, and invite and enjoin you by every consideration dear to the hearts of freemen and patriots, by the name and memory of your revolutionary fathers, and by the purity and sanctity of your domestic firesides, to rally to the standard of your State and country, and by every means in your power compatible with honorable warfare to drive back and expel the invaders from your land. I conjure you to be true and loyal to your country and her legal and constitutional authorities, and especially to be vigilant of the movements and acts of the enemy, so as to enable you to give the earliest authentic information to these headquarters or to officers under my command I desire to assure you that the utmost protection in my power will be extended to you all.

G. T BEAUREGARD,
Brigadier General, Commanding.

It is difficult to account for this remarkable proclamation, but it is most probable the general was suffering from non-action of the liver.

CHAPTER III

SAMUEL C MEANS GOES TO MARYLAND—GETS A COMMISSION TO RAISE A COMPANY OF CAVALRY—RECRUITING AT LOVETTS VILLE, ETC. — ELECTION OF OFFICERS — THE WATERFORD FIGHT

Samuel C. Means, a prominent citizen and a successful business man, owned and operated a splendid flour mill at Waterford, the largest in the county He and his brother (Noble B. Means) owned and conducted a large mercantile business at Point of Rocks, Md., and in addition to this was station agent of the B. & O. R. R. at the latter place. He wagoned the product of his mill to Point of Rocks, and shipped it thence by rail, to Baltimore market. There were very few men in Loudoun County doing a better business than Mr. Means. He went from his mill to his store daily, attending to his business as manufacturer, merchant, and railroad agent. The Confederates had repeatedly made very complimentary offers to Mr. Means, to enlist his sympathy for their cause, but without success. They next tried a system of coercion, with the same results. Finally he was notified that he must support the Confederacy or else he would be compelled to leave the State, and if he left the State, it would be presumed he was an enemy to the Confederacy, and his property would be confiscated To all their coaxing and threatening he emphatically said "No, gentlemen; you are waging a cruel and malicious war, without the slightest pretext, or excuse, upon the best government that ever existed. No, gentlemen, I will never take up arms against the United States; I will not be guilty of such disloyalty to my country." Mr. Means was a passionate and a positive man, and when presenting a statement would often grow emphatic, as was the case in this instance. The Confederates now determined to carry out their threats, and took a quantity of his flour for which they promised pay, but never paid They also took some of his stock. The crisis had come. Mr. Means went to Maryland about July 1, 1861, leaving his family behind. The Confederates took all his property that remained, consisting, in part, of 28 head of horses, 2 wagons, 42 head of hogs, large quantities of flour, meal, etc It should not be forgotten that it was no small sacrifice on his part, and also let it be well understood, it was for patriotism, for a lofty principle, that this self-sacrifice was made When Mr. Means left home he had no intention of going into the army, he so stated to his wife, and so wrote her after his arrival in Maryland. He had a brother in the rebel army and

did not wish to appear in a personal attitude on that
account. After the first battle of Bull 'Run, where the
Union army met with defeat, and the President called
for 300,000 troops, the question of duty presented its-
self so forcibly that he could not resist. He broke the
news first to his wife by letter, which almost broke her
heart. Mr Means made Point of Rocks his headquarters, attending to his private affairs.

It had been reported, during the fall of 1861, that
Mr Means had crossed the Potomac into Virginia, in dis-
guise, and visited his home in Waterford, and had been
concealed in his house for several days at a time. Capt.
William Meade's company of the Loudoun Cavalry
(Confederate), encamped in the latter village, received
special instructions to capture Mr. Means at all hazards.
A picket was stationed on Main Street, in full view
of the Means residence, with orders to rigidly guard
it. On October 18, at twelve o'clock, midnight, as
there was noticed a dim light going from room to
room, in the Means house, the officer of the guard
deemed it of sufficient importance to call Capt. Meade—
and there was also noticed a man approach the Means
residence and enter from the back door. This was
abundant evidence to Capt Meade that Mr. Means
was at home, and that the time to capture him had
arrived ; so with a squad of men he immediately surrounded the Means residence, and when all was ready
to enter and make the capture, suddenly the back
door opened and a person darted out through the garden
in a somewhat hurried manner. Capt. Meade and
Lieut. Len Giddings, with cocked revolver in each hand,
rushed like a Kansas cyclone upon this person, yelling,
" Surrender ! Surrender ! Sam Means, we have got you
this time " By the dashing and ferocious bravery of
these two heroes of many battles, the person was captured, slick and clean, and without a shot from either

side. The appetite for gore of these two battle-scarred
veterans was abundantly satisfied Capt. Means was
not at home The person thus captured was, it appears,
a female nurse attending upon a member of Mrs. Means'
family, who was busy making arrangements to entertain
a little stranger who had just come to town.

Capt. Meade well earned the title of "Granny Meade"

The 28th Pennsylvania Infantry, in command of
Colonel, afterwards Gen , John W. Geary, lay at Point
of Rocks, Md., and the 6th Independent Battery,
New York Artillery, lay at Brunswick. Mr. Means
spent much of his time with these two commands.
Col Geary was formerly a large real estate owner of
Loudoun, having owned a large interest in the Catoctin
Furnace tract, opposite Point of Rocks

These commands made repeated raids into Loudoun
during the fall and winter for the purpose of capturing
bands of rebels that were scouting in the county and
annoying Union people In December the 6th Independent New York Battery sent over into Virginia a
raiding party of about twenty-five men, who crossed at
Brunswick about 7 o'clock p m., went by Lovettsville,
capturing two rebels there, and, having traveled east-
ward, arrived opposite Point of Rocks about daylight,
where they surprised a rebel picket post, capturing
four and killing one, by the name of Orrison While
Mr. Means probably had nothing to do with these raids
(Mrs Means received a letter from her husband who
was in Baltimore the night of the raid), the Confederates accused him of their origin, and charged that the
damage inflicted on the rebels was directly traceable to
his hands. Consequently a reward of $5,000 was offered
by the Confederate authorities in Richmond for the head
of Samuel C Means, whom they characterized as the
renegade, Sam Means. The epithet renegade was in
exceeding bad taste. It should be remembered that

Mr. Means was simply one of a majority that refused to be defrauded out of his rights by the minority. A copy of the paper that contained the advertisement of a reward was sent to Mrs. Means from Richmond.

During January, 1862, Mr. Means received a letter from the Hon. Edwin M. Stanton, Secretary of War, requesting him to call at the War Department. On his arrival the Secretary offered him a commission, with the request that he would raise a command for the Union army. He informed the Hon. Secretary he would be pleased to accept the honor but at present he could not, but just as soon as he could adjust his private affairs he intended to offer his services in defence of the Union. In the mean time he transferred his business to his brother During the month of March there was a forward move of the army all along the Potomac from Washington to Cumberland. Col. Geary crossed the Potomac with his regiment, the 28th Pennsylvania, at Harper's Ferry, with Mr Means as guide, and took possession of Lovettsville and Waterford

This was the first time Mr. Means had returned to his home since he left it in July previous. He continued as guide to the army until May, when he returned to Washington and obtained a commission as captain, with instructions to recruit a company of cavalry to be known as the Independent Loudoun Guards Capt. Means was mustered into the United States service as captain, by Col. Dixon S. Miles, at Harper's Ferry, June 20, 1862 At the muster the name Rangers was substituted for Guards Headquarters were immediately established at Waterford, where recruiting was begun. The first name enrolled after that of Capt. Means was James A. Cox, of Hamilton, and that was followed closely by Charles F Anderson, Flemon B. Anderson, John S. Densmore, Jacob E. Boryer, Armstead Everhart, Luther W. Slater, Daniel M Keyes, James H. Corbin,

David E. B. Hough, Temple Fouch, John W. Forsythe, Joseph T. Cantwell, Thomas J. McCutcheon, Daniel J. Harper, Robert S. Harper, Henry C. Fouch, James W. Gregg and Milton S. Gregg, W. H. Angelow, Charles F. Atwell, J. W. and S Shackelford, Michael Mullen, James T. Wright, Samuel C. Hough, William Hough, Henry C. Hough. About July 1 the company moved camp to the Valley church, near Goresville, where about one dozen recruits were enrolled.

Joseph Waters was accidentally wounded by the discharge of a carbine while encamped here. This being our first man wounded in the company, the boys gathered around Joe uttering sympathetic bravos.

Secretary Stanton had given Capt. Means instructions to mount the company on horses that belonged to parties that had gone into the rebel army. While encamped at the church Capt. Means learned of a stranger at George Smith's residence, near Waterford, sick and apparently stranded. A detail was ordered, with instructions to bring this stranger to camp. He seemed to be much pleased at the change, but being an entire stranger, he was sent to Col. Miles at Harper's Ferry, where he was questioned at some length, when the oath of allegiance was administered to him. He then returned to our camp and offered himself as a recruit, giving the name of Charles A. Webster He was reticent as to his past history, but had evidently seen service before he came to us, being exceptionally well drilled in the cavalry tactics, was an excellent specimen of manhood, about five feet ten inches high, weighing about one hundred and eighty pounds, rather light complexioned, and about 25 years old ; very quick and active, a splendid shot, and wielded a sabre with great skill and effect.

Up to this time there was not a man in the company that understood the first principles of drilling ; so

Webster proved to be just the kind of a man that was needed, and he was immediately appointed our drill master.

It having been learned that some parties were engaged in forwarding rebel supplies from Baltimore and cross-ing the Potomac near Leesburg, a detail was made, with instructions to arrest those parties if possible. The squad started early in the morning, about 7th of July, crossing the Potomac at Edward's Ferry, where several parties were attempting to cross into Virginia with supplies for the Confederate army, consisting of arms, ammunition, clothing, etc. The parties thus engaged were arrested, and with the goods loaded on a canal boat and taken to Harper's Ferry and turned over to Col. Miles' command. The squad returned to the Valley church that evening, and having traveled about thirty-five miles that day, both men and horses were entirely exhausted.

About July 10 the company moved to Lovettsville and camped in the German Reformed church. This proved to be a very popular camp, being situated in the center of the German settlement, amongst friends. About twenty-five recruits enrolled their names here.

The company now numbered about fifty men, and was entitled to elect its officers. Capt. Means having been appointed captain, an election of officers was held, with the following result   1st Lieut., Luther W. Slater; 2d Lieut , Daniel M. Keyes ; Quartermaster, Charles F. Anderson; First Sergt., James A. Cox.

There were no other officers elected, or appointed, on this occasion. Charles E. Evard, of Leesburg, had been with the company for several weeks and was a modest candidate for first lieutenant. After this election he seemed to take little interest in the command, and finally left it entirely after the Waterford fight

About the 1st of August the company moved back to Waterford and camped in the Baptist church. The company continued to grow, and under the efficient drillmaster, Webster, began to obtain proficiency in the manual of arms. The company was now engaged in active scouting and succeeded in mounting all recruits on captured horses.

The Union army, under Gen. McClellan, had been compelled to retire from before Richmond, and the rebel army, somewhat elated over its dearly purchased temporary success, was moving northward. Quite a number had already returned to Loudoun and adjoining counties for the purpose of recruiting. Capt. Richard Simpson, of the 8th Va Reg Inf., with a detachment, was reported to be at Mount Gilead recruiting for that regiment. Capt. Cole, with a detachment of the 1st Md. P H B Cav, came down from Harper's Ferry on a contemplated raid to Middleburg and Upperville. Capt. Means and about thirty men joined the raid and suggested the route via Mount Gilead. The command left Waterford late in the afternoon, and camped for the night south of Clark's Gap. By making an early start an advance guard, consisting of Lieut. D. M Keyes, Charles A. Webster, James H. Beatty, M. S. Gregg, and perhaps two others, was hurried off in the direction of Mount Gilead and arrived at Capt. Simpson's rendezvous about 6 o'clock a m. The building was surrounded, but the birds had flown. Lieut Keyes ordered his men to proceed at once to Capt. Simpson's residence, located a half mile distant in a hollow. As they approached the house Capt. Simpson made his exit from the back door and ran across a field towards the timber He was commanded to halt, but kept running. Keyes, Webster, and Beatty fired several shots at him, one of which struck him in the leg, causing him to fall on his hands and knees, but he immediately jumped up and continued running towards the woods. Keyes gave chase across the field, while Webster, Beatty, Gregg, and others went around to head Simpson off at the woods. In the chase Keyes had emptied his revolver at Simpson, who had two revolvers, one of which contained several loads, and as Webster rode up he fired at Simpson, the ball taking effect in the body, bringing him to his knees, in which position he raised his revolver to shoot Webster. The latter, being very quick, wrenched one of Simpson's revolvers from his hand and with this weapon fired again, striking him, Simpson, in the neck, and from the effect of these wounds he soon died. Simpson was brave to recklessness Valuable Confederate papers were found on his person. Webster has been severely criticised, and perhaps to some extent justly, for the seemingly hasty methods used on this occasion; but Capt. Simpson had positively refused all demands made on him to surrender.

The advance guard waited for the column to come up, when the command proceeded via Aldie to Middleburg, where a squad of rebels was encountered and two captured.

The column moved on to Upperville where we arrived soon after daybreak This was a secession stronghold The women were even more pronounced in their views than the men, and grew eloquent in their denunciation of the Yankees.

Capt. Means and Capt Cole rode through the streets of the village, calling out to the citizens to prepare breakfast. The officers entered the same house, but much to their surprise no breakfast was visible. Capt Means asked for a cup to get a drink of milk No heed was given to this request. Finally, Ed Jacobs discovered some fine glassware on the sideboard and proceeded to pour out the milk for the temporary guests. This was more than the landlady could endure In her rage she exclaimed · "Why, the very idea of a Yankee drinking out of a cut glass!"

The command moved by way of Bloomfield, Purcell-ville, and Hamilton, back to camp at Waterford.

The entire Confederate army of Northern Virginia was now marching northward, threatening an invasion of Maryland. Our little camp at Waterford was somewhat exposed, we being the only Federal soldiers in this section of the State. Reports of the approach of the enemy were whispered around camp, but as the same news had been circulated for several weeks previous no particular importance was attached to the rumor. Capt Means had received private information that evening, August 26, which led him to believe that an attack that night was possible, although not probable.

The total strength of the company at this period was about fifty men, but a portion of that number were absent on a raid There were six public roads leading into the village, and a picket of four men was posted on each, taking just twenty-four men, leaving about twenty men in camp in the church, the latter being largely recruits, having quite recently joined fully half of the camp had been enrolled less than thirty days

Capt. Means was vigilant that night, endeavoring to learn of the accuracy of flying rumors, and visited the church as late as twelve o'clock midnight. When all seemed quiet he retired with his family, who lived in Waterford.

Lieut Luther W. Slater had been absent at his home for several days, sick, and had returned to camp that evening, partially recovered: Owing to the small number of men in camp First Sergeant Cox was having some difficulty in mounting the guard, and Lieut. Slater, who was a very popular officer, saw the embarrassment of the sergeant and cast himself in the breach by assuming double duty, acting as corporal of the guard as well as officer of the day.

A few minutes before three o'clock a. m , August 27, the enemy, consisting of Maj. E. V. White's 35th Bat-

Lieut. L. W. SLATER, Co. A.

talion, Virginia Cavalry, Ewell's Brigade, by being dismounted, and piloted by citizens and crossing fields, evaded our pickets and succeeded in reaching our camp unobserved.

The first apprehension we had of the approach of the enemy was an unusual noise, caused by the enemy, ostensibly for the purpose of drawing our men out of the church. The men rushed out in the front yard, where Lieut. Slater hastily formed them in line. A body of men could barely be recognized on the bank in front and on each side of the Virts' house and in the edge of the green corn. Lieut Slater's clear voice rang out on the early morning air in quick utterance, "Halt! Who comes there?" and in answer received a terrific volley from the carbines of the enemy, which our men gallantly returned, nothwithstanding over half had been wounded.

The rebels now took position behind buildings and in the green corn, and the Rangers fell back into the church. Lieut. Slater, although severely wounded, retained command until compelled by the loss of blood to relinquish that charge to Drillmaster Charles A. Webster, who continued the fight to its final termination, in a way that shed luster on his career as a brave and meritorious officer.

The rebels continued firing through the windows and the porch or vestibule of the church, a lath and plastered partition extending across the entire front The bullets poured through this barrier as they would through paper. The Rangers returned the fire as vigorously as circumstances would permit. After continuing the firing for about thirty minutes Maj. White sent in a flag of truce (by Mrs Virts) demanding a surrender, which was refused by Webster in rather emphatic language, that is not often heard in a church. The fight was continued, perhaps one hour longer, when the second flag of truce was sent in, making the same demand and sharing the same fate as the first, notwithstanding that one-half of the little band had been wounded and lay around in the church pews weltering in their blood, making the place look more like a slaughter pen than a house of worship

Our ammunition was almost exhausted, yet we hoped against hope that possibly assistance might reach us. The cry of the wounded for "Water! Water! Water!" when there was no water to be had, will never be forgotten The firing was kept up perhaps one hour longer, to about 6 30 or 7 o'clock, when the third flag of truce was sent in, making the same demands as the first and second.   At this time our ammunition was entirely exhausted, and as there was no possible way of replenishing that all-important article, Webster consulted Lieut. Slater as to what was best to do under the very precarious and unfortunate circumstances.   Lieut. Slater was lying in a pew on the north side of the church, being very weak from the loss of blood, which was still ebbing away, his underclothes being entirely saturated, and from the wound in his right temple his face was entirely covered with blood.   But possessing great physical endurance he was able to dictate a reply to Maj. White's demand for a capitulation, which was conditional.   The conditions as demanded by Slater and Webster were that all should be paroled and released on the spot , the officers to retain their side arms.

These terms were immediately accepted by Maj. White.

It was exceedingly fortunate for the Rangers at this juncture that the enemy made this third demand for a surrender, as it was impossible to have held out any longer ; and if he had only known it, he could have marched in and taken all prisoners and marched them off to Richmond Maj White asked that Webster meet him in the center of the street, under flag of truce, to arrange preliminaries. Webster drew his sword, and placing a pocket-handkerchief, belonging to John P. Hickman, on the point proceeded to the street to meet his antagonist. After exchanging greetings, White asked that Webster form his men in line in front of the church and surrender their arms, when all should be paroled and released   After all those that formed in line were paroled Maj White went in the church, where those who were severely wounded were paroled. On approaching Lieut. Slater, he remarked: "I am sorry to see you so dangerously wounded, Lieutenant"

Before the capitulation had taken place Maj. White sent a detachment down town, where our new arms and ammunition were stored, and got that which we were so badly in need of at the church.   After all had been paroled the enemy took the captured property and two prisoners, J. H. Corbin and Joseph Waters, and immediately left town, going south   Corbin and Waters were captured outside of the church, and not included in the terms of capitulation.

The casualties of this engagement were .

KILLED, Charles Dixon

WOUNDED : Lieut. Slater, five wounds—temple, shoulder, arm, breast, hand , a carbine ball passed through the top of his hat, but did no damage to his person.

Henry Dixon, mortally wounded, died five days later, ball passing through his bowels

Edward N. Jacobs, severely, ball passing through thigh bone.

James W. Gregg, in both arms.

D. M. Keyes, in neck

Henry C. Hough, in knee.

James A. Cox, in arm.

Robert W. Hough, in hand.

Charles A Webster, in side.

Colored man, company cook, in neck.

-- Henry Dixon was taken to the residence of Mr. Chal-

mers, where he was very tenderly cared for until death
relieved him of his sufferings

Lieut Slater was taken to the residence of Mr. Densmore, where he remained one week ; from there he was
removed to the residence of Mr George Alders, "Scotland," remaining there three weeks, when about ten of
his neighbors came and fastened a pole on each side of
his rocking chair, in which position they carried him
to his father's residence, near Taylortown. He was
kept there about two weeks, and removed to Gettysburg, Pa., where he remained until his wounds healed
sufficiently to allow him to travel.

While at Gettysburg he was again wounded, but by
no means painfully. While smarting under the sting
of "rebel bullets" he fell a victim to "Cupid's darts."
The "Guardian Angel" that so often and so tenderly
dressed his wounds and administered to his wants afterwards became Mrs. Slater.

Edward N. Jacobs was taken to the residence of John
B. Dutton

The others, whose wounds were painful, but not such
as to prevent them from traveling, were taken to their
various homes.

The following is the list of prisoners taken and paroled.

1st Lieut. L. W. Slater,	John W. Forsythe,
Charles A Webster,	T W Franklin,
James A Cox,	Samuel Fry,
Edward N Jacobs,	Joseph Fry,
John P Hickman,	R W. Hough,
Henry C Hough,	George W. Hough,
James W. Gregg,	S. J Cooper,
M H Best,	R S Harper,
Charles H. Snoots,	Charles L. Spring.
Samuel E. Tritapoe,	

After the first volley 2d Lieut. D. M. Keyes, Joseph T. Divine, Jacob E Boryer, and Charles White succeeded in making their escape by going down in the basement and jumping out of the rear window on the south side of the church.

The venerable Dr. Bond very kindly and very tenderly attended all the wounded

The author, who was in the church at the time, was not paroled He had enlisted three days previously, but was so short legged that a uniform could not be found small enough; but he had drawn one and taken it down town to Mrs Leggett's to have it made smaller, and was wearing a suit of citizens clothes, and was not taken for a soldier After the rest had been parolled he was recognized by Lieut R. C. Marlow, the latter probably supposing he was parolled

The casualties on the Confederate side, so far as known, were:

KILLED.—Lieut. Brooke Hayes.

Peter J Kabrich, mortally wounded, died a few days afterwards.

Those that were able to be moved were taken South , their number and names have never been learned.

While the fight was in progress Mr Kabrich ventured from behind the house and undertook to get one of the Rangers' horses that stood near the well While he was untying the animal Webster raised his carbine and fired and Kabrich fell, mortally wounded.

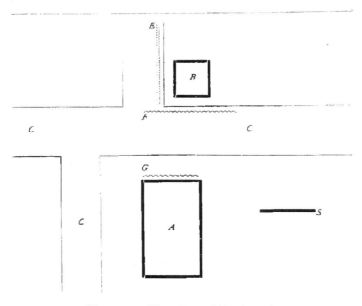

Diagram Showing Attack, etc.

A—Church.
B—Virt's House.
C—Street.
E—Direction of the Rebel approach.
F—Position of the Rebels when first volley.
G—Position of the Rangers when first volley.

Many of White's men and the Rangers had been schoolmates, and in some instances reared around the same fireside; one brother following the Confederate banner with a pitiable and delusive blindness, while the other brother stood firm in his allegiance to the Stars and Stripes.

In this fight brothers met. After the Rangers had been paroled Wm. Snoots, of White's command, wanted to shoot his brother Charles, who belonged to the Rangers, but was fittingly rebuked by his officers for such an unsoldierly and unbrotherly desire. Charles, who had been deprived of his arms, keenly felt the advantage his brother wanted to take, and modestly suggested to brother Bill that if he would unbuckle his arms and lay them aside he, Charles, would wipe up the earth with the cowardly cur in less than two minutes.

The official records fail to show any reports of this engagement from either side, the only mention made is the following telegram from General Wool to Secretary Stanton

"HARPER'S FERRY, VA., *August 27, 1862.*

" Cole's Maryland Cavalry returned from Waterford The enemy, under Capt. White, by crossing fields and avoiding the pickets, attacked twenty-three of Means' men in a church at daybreak this morning, who fought as long as they had ammunition. Two privates killed, 1st and 2d lieutenants and six privates wounded, fifteen surrendered on parole, two engaged in killing Mr. Jones carried off to Richmond to be held as hostages; also, thirty horses and all the arms of the company except those on picket. The enemy lost six killed and nine wounded

"JOHN E. WOOL,
" *Maj. Gen., Commanding.*"

J H. Corbin and Joseph Waters were taken to Culpeper Court House, where the latter was paroled, Corbin was placed in prison, charged with killing a Mr Jones, which occurred previous to Corbin's enlistment, the latter remained in irons about ten days, when a loyal citizen of that place assisted him in making his escape

The Confederates, under command of Maj White, with White's command, and Capt. Randolph, of the Black Horse Cavalry (4th Va), and Capt Gallaher, of Ashby's Cavalry, the latter as scouts, the entire cavalcade numbering perhaps two hundred, left the North Fork of the Rappahannock River August 24, and marched through Fauquier County, entering Loudoun near Middleburg, taking the Mountain Road, and marched direct to Waterford, arriving about 2 o'clock a. m , August 27, dismounting near Robert Hollingsworth's barn, where the horses were left, and marched direct to the church and made the attack   The command was piloted by about a half dozen citizens—Henry Ball, J Simpson, and others, who lived in Loudoun

A few days before the fight there came to our camp at Waterford a Mr Robertson and joined the company , a very quiet fellow, but apparently had his eyes open. An entire stranger to all, the only person he seemed to cultivate the acquaintance of was Joseph T. Divine, whom he asked to accompany him to the residence of Gen Robert L Wright, near Wheatland. He remained around camp until about the time of the fight, when he disappeared forever from the company

It is believed that Mr Robertson was a Confederate spy and belonged to the command of Capt. Gallaher, who accompanied White on this raid, and that he afterwards joined White's company, as a man by that name joined that command in 1862.

CHAPTER IV.

The Leesburg Fight—The Confederate Army Invades Maryland

After the Waterford fight the Rangers established their camp at Catoctin Furnace, guarding the fords of the Potomac. The strength of the company was now reduced to about thirty-five men

September 1 the command started on a raid through Loudoun At Hillsborough we attacked and routed a body of White's Cavalry, capturing two prisoners and several horses and equipments. The prisoners captured were present at Waterford four days previous. Our captives and horses were sent to Harper's Ferry. We were joined with parts of two companies of Cole's

Cavalry, numbering 125 men, and proceeded in the direction of Leesburg. The command halted for the night at the palatial farm-house of Gen. Robert L Wright, C. S A., Commanding the Militia of Loudoun The General always had plenty for the hungry, and both man and beast fared well that night.

The next morning, September 2, the column started for Leesburg, going by way of the Valley church, there to perform the last sad rites over the body of our late comrade, Henry Dixon, who was mortally wounded at Waterford August 27th, and died September 1st.

By some misunderstanding as to the time of the funeral, we arrived at the church about two hours before the remains After the funeral the march was continued to Leesburg, where we arrived about twelve o'clock We captured the enemy's picket. Charles F. Atwell, Peter Miles, and George W. Baker were put on picket south of town, and Cole's Cavalry picketed the other roads leading out.

In about twenty minutes the picket on the Edward's Ferry Road was driven in by a large body of the enemy's cavalry We met them with several volleys from our revolvers. Peter Miles' horse was shot dead, falling at the corner of the Court House Square, where Miles was captured

Secession sentiment was practically unanimous in Leesburg, and Union troops would be at great disadvantage in the streets in battle array, consequently Cole and Means fell back on the Point of Rocks Road to the Mile Hill, there entered a field on the west side of the road and formed in line of battle, facing Leesburg.

The enemy also halted and entered a field on the east side of the road and formed, taking position behind some wheat stacks. The Federal line now advanced towards the enemy in the direction of Leesburg As we approached the top of Mile Hill a terrific yell was raised in our rear by a heavy column of the enemy, approaching from the direction of Big Spring, charging battalion front. We were completely surrounded, our only hope lay in breaking through their lines.

Our column charged by right flank, and we succeeded in extricating ourselves from the very perilous situation in which we were placed by overwhelming numbers.

As both parties had emptied their revolvers and there was no time to reload, sabers were drawn and freely used. We fell back in as good order as was possible under the circumstances, the enemy pressing us hard for about six miles, to near Waterford.

Several of Means' and Cole's men received sabre wounds in breaking through the rebel lines.

This force of the enemy proved to be the 2d Virginia Cavalry, commanded by Col. Mumford It was Gen. Lee's advance, moving northward, preparatory to their first invasion of Maryland, which occurred three days later, crossing at Edward's and White's Ferries, about three miles from Leesburg.

As our command entered town this regiment lay east of the village, near where is now located the depot Upon learning of our presence and numbers they divided their forces into two columns, one going north of the village and taking a concealed position on the Point of Rocks Road, the route by which we entered, the other column to charge in town by the Edward's Ferry Road and drive us out (the Point of Rocks Road thus placing us between their two columns) and crush us Their scheme was not as successfully carried out as it was cunningly planned.

In this fight our loss was.

KILLED —Frank Morman.

WOUNDED —Armistead Everhart, shot through right knee, bone badly broken

Jacob Long, shot through right thigh, leg badly broken.

Jacob E. Boryer, shot through left hip, bone badly broken, and sabre cut on right shoulder.

Jacob Cordell, shot through neck

George W. Baker, shot through right shoulder.

S. Shackelford, shot through left foot.

PRISONERS.—Armistead Everhart, Jacob Long, Jacob Cordell, Charles Baker, Peter Miles, William Shoemaker, George Welch.

Charles Baker, George Welch, Peter Miles, and William Shoemaker, not wounded, were sent direct to Richmond

George W Baker, Armistead Everhart, Jacob Cordell, and Jacob Long, being severely wounded, were kept in the hospital one week at Leesburg, then removed to Winchester, where they were kept one week Jacob Long and Armistead Everhart, whose wounds were dangerous and whose recovery seemed doubtful, were paroled and left there.

The remainder of the wounded were removed to Staunton, were they were kept one week, and then sent to Richmond.

George Welch, Charles Baker, Peter Miles, and William Shoemaker were placed in Castle Thunder, charged with violating their parole The charges were totally false, as neither had ever been captured before. Baker, Miles, and Shoemaker starved to death there. When Richmond was captured, in April, 1865, George Welch was found confined in a dungeon, and was released, but so near death's door that he was totally unfit for service. He came back to the command at Harper's Ferry, where he was discharged, in May, 1865, and his friends have not heard from him since

George W. Baker returned to the company in May, 1863; in August following was placed on detached duty at Gen Crook's headquarters, as courier, where he served until the close of the war

We believe Cole's Cavalry suffered a proportionate loss—four killed and forty wounded—two of the killed being commissioned officers.

The Confederates also lost heavily. Their dead and wounded were sent away, Maj. Davis, one of their leading officers, being killed.

The Waterford and the Leesburg engagements came in such close succession, before the company had attained proficiency in discipline and drill, that they almost broke up the organization. It may be stated here that these two engagements did to a very large extent interfere with the future usefulness of the command

If the results of these two battles had been favorable to the Rangers it is more than probable that a full regiment would have been recruited under their banner.

Charles E Evard, of Leesburg, had received instructions to raise a company for the command, but recruiting had received such a set back that he abandoned the effort.

After the Leesburg encounter the company numbered less than twenty men for immediate duty This handfull established its camp at Point of Rocks, Md , guarding the fords of the Potomac from the Monocacy River to Brunswick and bearing dispatches from Col. H B. Banning, 87th Ohio Infantry, from Point of Rocks to Col Miles at Harper's Ferry.

September 6 the Rangers moved to Harper's Ferry. September 5 the enemy, commanded by Gen. R. E. Lee, invaded Maryland for the first time, crossing the Potomac at Edward's and Noland's Ferry, and by the 7th Lee encamped at Frederick City.

From the beginning of hostilities Maryland had assumed a doubtful attitude towards the Union

Gov. Hicks wanted to make the State neutral, and

protested against Fedeial troops passing through the
State.　He also made the surprising suggestion that
the British Minister at Washington arbitrate between
the North and the South, that the shedding of blood
might be averted ; but, finally, the governor came out
for the Union in language that could not be misunderstood.　He proved to be one of President Lincoln's
staunchest supporters, and rendered valuable service to
his country and its flag.　Up to this time, in Maryland,
if a citizen of the State insisted on going with the
South he must leave his home and go South, now the
South had come to him

Frederick was the home of that " Brigadier," Bradley
T. Johnson, and was also supposed to contain many who
only wished for an opportunity to don the gray.　September 8 Gen. Lee issued a somewhat bombastic proclamation to the Marylanders, perhaps somewhat prosaic
for war times.　However, we shall risk the reader's
patience by reproducing a few of the "spell-binding"
passages:

"The people of the South have brought liberty and
protection to your homes　They have long wished to
aid you in throwing off this foreign yoke of oppression,
and to enable you again to enjoy the inalienable rights
of freemen, and restore the independence and sovereignty of your State."

Recruiting offices were opened and Marylanders invited to cast their lot with the Southern Confederacy,
by shouldering a musket and following the "Bonny
Blue Flag "

The response to this proclamation was a sad disappointment.　It was humiliating in the extreme to
Gen. Lee.　Instead of the thousands that were expected
to rally around the standard of secession, probably less
than one hundred thought so little of their lives as to
risk them in defence of such a miserable cause.

The truth is that the people of western Maryland, with few exceptions, were loyal to the National Government, and did not hesitate to " prove their faith by their works." Thousands of them died that posterity might enjoy the benefits of a free and undivided country.

Frederick was an intensely loyal city. One of the shining examples of its patriotic fervor was in the person of that patron saint, Barbara Freitchie, who waved defiance in the face of that alleged Christian soldier, Stonewall Jackson. She died a few months after this event, and over her grave in the Frederick cemetery is a marble slab with the simple but impressive words " Barbara Freitchie." This inscription will tell the story of her patriotism to future generations. Humanity will never tire of reading the immortal poem of Whittier, the Quaker poet

BARBARA FREITCHIE'
J G. WHITTIER

Up from the meadows rich with corn,
Clear in the cool September morn,
The clustered spires of Frederick stand
Green walled by the hills of Maryland

Round about them orchards sweep,
Apple and peach-tree fruited deep,
Fair as a garden of the Lord
To the eyes of the famished rebel horde.

On that pleasant morn of the early fall,
When Lee marched over the mountain wall,
Over the mountains, winding down,
Horse and foot into Frederick town,

Forty flags with their silver stars,
Forty flags with their crimson bars,
Flapped in the morning wind; the sun
Of noon looked down and saw not one

Up rose old Barbara Frietchie then,
Bowed with her four score years and ten
Bravest of all in Frederick town,
She took up the flag that men hauled down.

In her attic window the staff she set,
To show that one heart was loyal yet
Up the street came the rebel tread,
Stonewall Jackson riding ahead

Under his slouched hat left and right
He glanced—the old flag met his sight
"Halt!" The dust-browned rank stood fast;
"Fire!" Out blazed the rifle blast

It shivered the window, pane and sash;
It rent the banner with seam and gash
Quick as it fell, from the broken staff
Dame Barbara snatched the silken scarf

She leaned far out on the window sill,
And shook it forth with a royal will.
"Shoot, if you must, this old gray head,
But spare your country's flag!" she said

A shade of sadness, a blush of shame
Over the face of the leader came,
The noblest nature within him stirred
To life at that woman's deed and word

"Who touches a hair of you gray head
Dies like a dog! March on!" he said.
All day long thro' Frederick street
Sounded the tread of marching feet,

All day long that free flag tossed
Over the head of the rebel host,
Ever its torn folds rose and fell
On the loyal winds that loved it well,

And through the hill gaps sunset light
Shone over it with a warm good night.
Barbara Frietchie's work is o'er,
And the rebel rides on his raids no more.

Honor to her! and let a tear
Fall, for her sake, on Stonewall's bier.
Over Barbara Fritchie's grave
Flag of Freedom and Union, wave!

Peace and order and beauty draw
Round thy symbol of light and law,
And ever the stars above look down
On thy stars below in Frederick town!

About twelve years after the war some ghoulish persons attempted to break the force of Whittier's poem by declaring it was fiction, etc

They had just as well claim Paul Revere's ride was a myth, or Phil Sheridan's black horse was a hoax.

Dame Barbara was there with her "silken scarf," and did not hesitate to wave it in the face of treason on all occasions.

Frederick was also the birth place of Francis Scott Key, the author of "The Star Spangled Banner."

While the rebels were placing this proclamation before the citizens, their soldiers were plundering the stores and driving off the cattle   The "liberty and protection" that Gen. Lee claimed to have brought was evidently not the kind the Marylanders enjoyed.

Gen Lee's stay in Frederick was brief, as he remained there but three days dishing out his "liberty and protection" to the citizens.   Before he left, however, he issued an order directing the future movements of his army in the State, a copy of which fell into the hands of Gen. McClellan two days later, September 12

It will be remembered that the Federal troops, under command of Col. D H. Miles, were still in possession of Harper's Ferry.   The enemy could not hope for any permanent success while this force was allowed to menace their rear, and issued the following order for its dislodgement

Gen. Jackson, with three divisions, his own, Ewell's, and A. P. Hill's, was directed to march via Boonsboro, cross the Potomac River below Williamsport, capture the Federal forces under Gen White at Martinsburg and attack Harper's Ferry from Bolivar Heights.

Capt. JAMES W. GRUBB, Co. B.

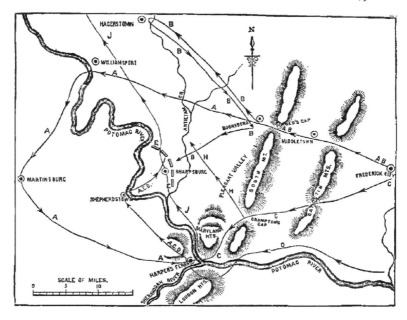

REBEL MOVEMENTS ON HARPER'S FERRY AND ANTIETAM.

By Permission of "Siege and Capture of Harper's Ferry." By W. H. Nichols, 3d.

  A A—Jackson's march from Frederick to Harper's Ferry.
  C C—McLaw's and Anderson's march from Frederick to Maryland
       Heights.
  D D—Walker's march from the Monocacy to Loudoun Heights.
  A C D—Enemy's line of march from Harper's Ferry to Antietam.
  B B—Longstreet's march to Antietam.
  H H—Franklin's march from Pleasant Valley to Antietam.
    J J—Line of march of the Union Cavalry escaping from Harper's
       Ferry before the surrender.
  E E—Lee's line of battle during the battle of Antietam.

Gen. Longstreet, accompanied by Gen. Lee, was to
halt at Boonsboro with the trains. Gen. McLaws, with
two divisions, his own and Anderson's, was to move direct and ascend the mountain at Crampton's Pass and
attack Maryland Heights Gen. Walker, with one division, was to cross the Potomac River at Noland's
Ferry and march via Hillsboro and attack Harper's

Ferry from Loudoun Heights. The three armies left
Frederick the 10th and were to be at their appointed
places the evening of the 12th, to open the attack the
morning of the 13th, and after the place with its garrison was captured, all to be reunited again at Boonsboro.
The programme of Gen. Lee was carried out with but
two exceptions : Gen. Walker was prevented from crossing the river at Noland's Ferry by Gen. McClellan, but
crossed 4 miles further up, at Point of Rocks, and the
entire Confederate army was reunited at Sharpsburg
in place of Boonsboro.

This was the golden opportunity of Gen. McClellan's
life. The entire plan of his adversary was completely
revealed to him ; he should have fallen on Gen. Lee's
divided Army and defeated it in detail. There was
absolutely nothing to prevent it. All authorities and
critics agree on this point. The distance from Fred-
crick to Harper's Ferry is about 20 miles. The Confederates marched it in about two days, while Gen.
McClellan made only 6 miles a day.

HARPER'S FERRY.

CHAPTER V.

THE ATTACK UPON HARPER'S FERRY—THE CAVALRY CUT
THEIR WAY OUT—CAPITULATION OF THE POST—BATTLE OF
ANTIETAM

The troops at Harper's Ferry were parts of the First
and Eighth Corps, and stationed as follows, Col. Dixon
H Miles, of the Regular army, in command :

On Bolivar Heights—39th New York, 111th New
York, 115th New York, 15th Indiana Battery, 60th
Ohio, 9th Vermont, 126th New York, Potts' Battery,
Company F, 32d Ohio, 12th New York, four Companies
87th Ohio, Rigby's First Indiana Battery, and Company
A, 5th New York Heavy Artillery The forts contained
twelve howitzers. On the hill next to the Shenandoah
River were stationed four Parrotts and twelve pounders ;
the latter commanded the Charlestown pike and the
approaches from Sandy Hook

There was stationed on Maryland Heights—32d Ohio,
1st Maryland P. H. B., a detachment of 5th New York
Heavy Artillery, two companies First Maryland Cavalry,
Seventh Squadron, Rhode Island Cavalry, and about
twelve men of the Loudoun Rangers. The heights
contained some of the best artillery in the service ;
heavy siege guns, two ten-inch Dahlgrens, one fifty-
pound gun, and four twelve-pound howitzers. The
Dahlgrens could easily destroy a battery four miles
away.

At Sandy Hook there were five companies of the
1st Maryland P. H B., eight companies of the 87th
Ohio, three pieces of Potts' Artillery, and Cole's Maryland Cavalry.

The forces at Shepherdstown, Col. Downey in command These consisted of three companies of the 3d

Maryland P H B., and the 8th New York Cavalry ; and Gen. White was at Martinsburg with the 125th New York, 65th Illinois Infantry, 12th Illinois Cavalry, and Phillipp's 2nd Illinois Battery. These troops had all retired to Harper's Ferry, making the entire force about 14,500.

Gen. White was now the ranking officer, but waived his right to command in favor of Col Miles.

The Confederates began shelling the place from Loudoun Heights Saturday morning McLaws attacked Maryland Heights with infantry, where the fighting continued heavy during the forenoon, the enemy meeting with a repulse. A verbal order was received late in the evening by Col Ford, purporting to come from Col. Miles, to abandon the heights. This order seemed so unreasonable that it was obeyed with reluctance Capt. McGrath, who was in command of the siege guns, cried like a child when ordered to spike and abandon his Dahlgrens, and he remarked to Col. Ford that it was the act of a traitor to either give or obey such an order Saturday night all the troops stationed on Maryland Heights and Sandy Hook were withdrawn to the Ferry and took position on Bolivar Heights Strange to say, the Confederates did not take possession of Maryland Heights for nearly twenty-four hours after it was abandoned The next day (Sunday), about noon, Maj. Wood returned to Maryland Heights with four. companies without opposition, and brought back four guns and large quantities of ammunition.

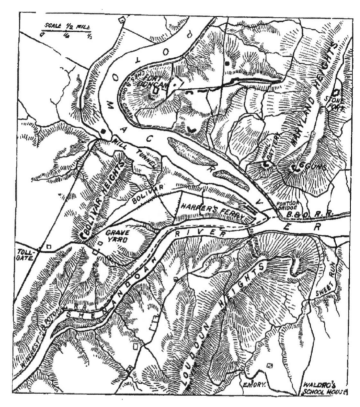

HARPER'S FERRY AND SURROUNDING COUNTRY.

Before the Loudoun Rangers retired from Maryland Heights Saturday night, Capt. Means marched his men into a thicket of woods, and with pick and shovel began digging a hole about two by four feet. Many were the conjectures as to the object of this hole in the ground. When completed, Zack Robison and Webb Miner lifted a box from the wagon containing the company books and papers, together with Capt. Means' papers, that he did not want to fall into the hands of the enemy, and buried them, spreading dry leaves and brush over the spot to prevent detection. Then the company retired to Harper's Ferry with the other troops.

Saturday night, Col Miles ordered Capt Russell, with ten cavalrymen, to go out and endeavor to reach Gen. McClellan's headquarters and inform the General of the condition of affairs, and that the place did not contain rations for more than four days. After several encounters with the enemy's pickets, Capt Russell arrived at Gen. McClellan's headquarters, near Frederick, at 9 o'clock Sunday morning.

Early Sunday morning, Graham's Battery, on Camp Hill, Harper's Ferry, opened on the enemy's batteries on Loudoun Heights The latter did not reply until the afternoon In the mean time the enemy succeeded in placing heavy guns on Maryland Heights, and about 4 o'clock there began a heavy cannonading from Maryland and Loudoun Heights, on Col Miles' position on Bolivar Heights. The enemy's guns being much higher than ours were, of course, more effective

Sunday night closed with every possible advantage in favor of the enemy, every commanding position having been surrendered to them without any apparent contest, and it must have been evident to every one, from Col Miles down to the high private in the rear rank, that it was only a question of time, and a short time, too, when every man and gun at Harper's Ferry would be in possession of the enemy.

The next thing, then, was to save as much from the debris as was possible The cavalry was stationed on the island where was formerly located the Hall Rifle Works This arm of the service was of no use in the defense of the place. In fact, it was a hindrance, as it consumed large quantities of rations and forage which were absolutely needed for those that were useful in defense of the garrison.

The Confederate authorities had previously offered a large reward for Capt. S C. Means, who well knew if he surrendered with the place what would be his doom ; he therefore concluded he could not afford to assume such risk, and immediately began to organize a force of cavalry that would endeavor to cut its way out When the matter was first suggested to Col. Miles he was much opposed to it, stating that he preferred to keep the entire forces together. Capt Means preferred to go out with Col. Miles' approval, but to go out if he disapproved When it was found that the effort was warmly seconded by Col. Davis, Eighth N Y Cavalry, Col. Voss, Twelfth Ill. Cavalry, Maj. Cole (Cole's Md Cavalry), Maj. Corliss, Seventh Squadron, R. 1. Cavalry, then Col. Miles consented and issued an order accordingly. Capt Means suggested that the cavalry cross the Shenandoah River, file left, taking the river road, around Short Hill Mountain, through Lovettsville and Leesburg, crossing the Potomac on the Chain Bridge and entering Washington through Georgetown Col. Davis, Eighth N Y Cavalry, wanted to go out by passing up the south bank of the Potomac, crossing at Boteler's Ford. Both of these routes were open to objection, as the march would be through the enemy's country all the way out. Either Col Cole or Capt Summers suggested the route that was finally adopted, as set forth in Col. Miles' order.

About 9 o'clock p. m. Sunday, September 14th, 2,000 cavalry crossed the Potomac on the pontoon bridge, filed left, crossed the Chesapeake and Ohio Canal, and took the Antietam furnace road. We had not proceeded more than a mile when the enemy's pickets were encountered, with the ultimatum "Halt ! Who comes there ?" Above the clatter of hoofs and the turbulent Potomac dashing against the rocks was heard the clear voice of Lieut. Green, of Company A, Cole's Cavalry, ring out, "The advance of Stuart's Cavalry !" This answer was given to deceive , it was intended to thwart the vigilance of the picket, who seemed completely dumbfounded as we rushed past. A piece of artillery was in position by the roadside , a few shots were fired, but did no damage to our side. As we approached Antietam Creek we suddenly rushed on the enemy, who were cooking supper. Success now depended on bold-ness and audacity, and we rode pell-mell over them, scattering their fires, roasting ears, and rye coffee in every direction, pouring a volley into the darkness as we passed Their officers could be heard commanding, "Fall in! Fall in!" It was now every man for him-self, and the "Devil take the hindmost." The column would occasionally halt where Cole's Cavalry was ac-quainted and endeavor to obtain information concern-ing the enemy, as to location and numbers We passed through Sharpsburg about 3 o'clock a. m.

A halt was made here for a few minutes, principally to rest the horses and obtain information The enemy's pickets were encountered quite often for about 15 miles. Just after leaving Sharpsburg a small body of the enemy's cavalry was encountered, which we charged battalion front, and scattered them in the darkness. We were enabled by the enemy's bivouac fires to avoid running into large numbers. The direction was now changed considerably to the west of north to avoid Lee's army, that was concentrating near Sharpsburg. Just about daybreak, Monday morning, was heard a rumbling of wagons in our immediate front ; a halt was made to "take sounding." Imagine our consternation, which was finally turned into delight when it was found to be Gen. Longstreet's ammunition train, and escort of about 200 cavalry. Col. Voss ordered the entire column to form and charge, when about 2,000 men swooped down on the train and captured it with but slight resistance.

It was a valuable trophy, consisting of about 80 wagons and 200 prisoners. The wagons contained every conceivable kind of death-dealing missile to fire from a cannon. The drivers were very aggravating and obstinate when they were made prisoners, and ordered to change the direction of their teams, some of them endeavored to upset their wagons by running them into fences, etc. A few of the most refractory were prodded with the sabre, which brought the balance to immediate subjection. One case caused considerable annoyance and also cost the driver his life , he ran his team into the fence, completely wrecking it. As no time was to be lost getting it out, some of the boys jumped over the fence, gathered a few armsful of straw from a stack near by, placed it under the wagon, set fire to it and left it to the mercy of the flames As the column moved forward, perhaps 200 yards, there was heard a terrific explosion, equalling a thousand batteries masked and opened on our rear. Col. Voss immediately put the column in line to resist a supposed attack from Longstreet's army that was near. As the smoke cleared away the ground was strewn with fragments of shell and splinters of a wagon—the attack was over.

The wagon that was stranded in the fence and set fire to was loaded with shell, and when the flames reached the powder it exploded, with a noise equal to a hundred Dahlgrens, such as we had left on Maryland Heights.

We took these wagons and prisoners into Greencastle that morning by 9 o'clock, where the citizens gave us a royal reception and a bountiful breakfast '

These wagons had originally belonged to Uncle Sam and were captured from Gen. Pope's army at Second Manassas, just fourteen days previous

Our loss on this raid was probably not over 75 men. Several of that number came in and reported to their commands in the next few days. Col. B. F. Davis,

Eighth N. Y Cavalry, received a special compliment
for bravery exhibited on this raid, and he was recom-
mended for promotion.   He was unfortunately killed
at Beverly Ford, Va., June 9, 1863, while leading a
brigade of cavalry against the enemy.

We believe the conception of the raid belongs to
Capt. Means and Charles A. Webster, of the Loudoun
Rangers, while a large share of the successful execution
belongs to Cole's (Md.) Cavalry.

The column was piloted through by a loyal citizen of
Bolivar, by the name of Burkett.

While the various officers did their duty nobly, the
private soldiers are justly entitled to their full share
of credit, for without them it would have been a disastrous failure.

After reporting at Greencastle, Capt Means marched
his men to Baltimore, where he was summoned to report in person to Gen. Wool, giving a full account of
the cavalry making their escape from Harper's Ferry.
He also obtained horses there for those of his men who
were dismounted.   The next day we went to Ellicott's
Mills, when those that became separated from the
company a few days before we left the Ferry joined us,
consisting of Joe Divine, Dan Harper, Jeff McCutcheon,
and others.   The entire command marched to Frederick,
and on past Middletown and Boonsboro, where we met
the first ambulances bringing in the wounded from
Antietam   The Rangers were assigned to duty on the
right, bearing dispatches, and did good service during
the battle, when they captured probably four times
their own number of rebel stragglers from Lee's army.

STREET SCENE, HARPER'S FERRY.
[By permission of B. & O. R. R.]

We will now return to Harper's Ferry. Monday morning, September 15, the enemy opened their batteries on Col. Miles' position from Maryland and Loudoun Heights, and in front of Bolivar Heights. The cannonading was terrific and very disastrous to the beleagured army. The situation was made more galling by the fact that the Federal guns were not supplied with long-range ammunition. Our batteries on Camp Hill returned the fire of the enemy in a vigorous

manner, but with little effect. Col Miles called his
officers together about 9 a m , as a council of war, and
after a somewhat protracted conference they voted
that resistance under the circumstances was useless
While this body was in session, Gen. White ordered
the massing of his batteries on Bolivar Heights, preparatory to making a charge on the enemy's position.
When Col. Miles learned of this he countermanded the
order.   At 11 a m. Col Miles ordered a white flag
to be displayed where the Stars and Stripes had previously floated, and suggested Gen. White to meet Gen.
Jackson and arrange terms of capitulation.   Owing to
the rain that morning there was a heavy fog, which
prevented the enemy from recognizing the flag of truce,
and they continued firing   It is claimed that a shell
from one of these guns struck Col. Miles, severely wounding him, from the effects of which he died the next day.

It is perhaps just to those who survived the unfortunate affair to state that the wounding of Col Miles by
the enemy is denied.   It has been asserted by those
who witnessed the affair that the fatal shot was fired
by an Indiana battery.

Col. Miles would not permit the destruction of any
Government property , he permitted it to fall into the
hands of the enemy in good condition   He did not
destroy the pontoon bridge after evacuating Maryland
Heights, as he should have done ; it was left for the
Confederates to use, and by the use of it Gen Stonewall Jackson was enabled to put his army on the field
of Antietam at least eight hours earlier than would
have otherwise been possible.

Col Miles' son-in-law was an officer on the staff of
Stonewall Jackson

The enemy's loss in killed and wounded, as reported
by themselves, was about 500. The Federal loss in killed
and wounded, strange to say, was not over half of that
of the enemy.

By the surrender of Harper's Ferry the enemy came into possession of about 12,000 prisoners, 47 pieces of artillery, 13,000 small arms, and large quantities of supplies

The prisoners were paroled and marched to Annapolis, Md.

Military circles were very much agitated over this unfortunate affair The public press also contained criticisms that somewhat reflected on the patriotism and courage of prominent officers that were present. Gen. Julius White, the ranking officer present, but who waived his right to Col. Miles, keenly felt that his own military record would most probably be questioned, and addressed the following letter to the Adjutant General

> "ANNAPOLIS, MD,
> "*September* 23, 1862

" Brig. Gen. LORENZO THOMAS,
> "*Adjt Gen*, *U. S A.*

"GENERAL . I have the honor to state that in my judgment the public interests require an investigation into the causes of the recent surrender of Harper's Ferry with the garrison stationed there, and do therefore respectfully request that a court of inquiry be ordered for the purpose

" I am, general, very respectfully,
> · your obedient servant,
> > "JULIUS WHITE,
> > "*Brig. Gen*, *U S A.*

A court of inquiry was convened in Washington, September 25, 1862, and composed of the following persons :

Gen. D Hunter,	Capt Donn Piatt, A. A. G ,
Gen. G. Cadwalader,	Capt. F. Ball, Jr., A. D. C.
Gen. C. C Augur,	Col J Holt, Judge Advocate

The court remained in session forty days and examined twenty-eight witnesses. The testimony given is very voluminous, covering several hundred closely-printed pages. Capt Means' testimony is given in full. For the entire testimony of all other witnesses the reader is referred to series 1, vol. 19, part 1, Official Records of the Rebellion.

SIGNAL STATION ON LOUDOUN HEIGHTS.
[By permission of B. & O. R. R.]

Capt. S. C MEANS, called by the Government, and sworn and examined as follows :

By the JUDGE ADVOCATE :

Question. What is your position in the military service ?

Answer. Captain of cavalry.

Question. In what regiment?

Answer. An independent company. We are not attached to any regiment at all.

Question. Were you at Harper's Ferry during the late events there which resulted in its surrender?

Answer. Yes, sir, up to Sunday night I was not there when the surrender was made.

Question. Did you leave on Sunday night?

Answer. Yes, sir

Question. Under what circumstances?

Answer. Well, when Maryland Heights were surrendered, I just thought we might just as well surrender the Ferry And I knew I would be hanged if I was caught.

Question. You are a Virginian?

Answer. Yes, sir. I thought if I could get out I would, and I invited all who wished to follow me to follow me; and there were a great many that did.

Question Did you escape with the large body of cavalry, or in the advance?

Answer. I was in advance of the whole body.

Question You encountered no difficulty in effecting your escape?

Answer We had some little skirmishing along the route; nothing serious

Question. Are you well acquainted with the geography and topography of that region?

Answer On the Virginia side I am. On the Marylany side I can not say that I am, very well. I am well acquainted, but not very well. There are a great many passes there I do not understand.

Question. Will you give the Commission your judgment as to whether the infantry could have effected their escape the night the cavalry cut their way through?

Answer. I do not think there would have been any difficulty in the world.

Question. You think they could have passed over the road you passed over?

Answer. Yes, sir; the infantry could have done it, the artillery could not. The infantry could have

done it well and easy. It was through the mountain ;
a rough road   It would have been bad for artillery to
have gotten over, it is very true, but infantry could have
done it.

By the COURT

Question. Why could not the artillery have passed
over the road ?
Answer. The artillery could not have taken that
road on account of the noise they would have made
I have no doubt they could have got over it.   The only
obstruction we met with was when we met with the
ammunition train of Longstreet   We heard a considerable noise, and drew up in line of battle in a field,
tore down the fences, and got back into a field   But we
had no skirmishing , they surrendered at once   When
we ordered the train to halt, they halted and gave themselves up at once.

By General WHITE .

Question. You have stated that you thought there
would have been no difficulty in the infantry going out
at the time you did. How long, in your opinion,
would it have taken the infantry to have crossed the
Potomac ?
Answer I think there were, perhaps, 10,000 men
there, and it would, perhaps, have taken them three
hours, I think.
Question. After crossing, how long, suppose there had
been no interruption whatever—how long would it
have taken them to have marched where they would
have been perfectly clear of danger of attack and being
surrounded by the enemy ?
Answer. Well, sir, three hours more would have taken
them out.
Question. When you say "out," do you mean clear
around the enemy's left flank ?
Answer. Yes, sir , I mean entirely out of their lines
Question And how far would that have been ?
Answer Twelve miles.
Question Is not that more than three hours' march ?

Rattling Spring.

Answer. A forced march could have done it. "Stonewall" Jackson could have done it, I know.

Question. You say you had some little skirmishing with the enemy?

Answer. Very little, we expected to have a skirmish with the guard that was with the ammunition train, but they showed no fight; they surrendered

Question. You had some with the pickets?

Answer. Occasionally a shot; not a skirmish, but a shot now and then.

Question With infantry, marching as a column of infantry would, what is your opinion as to their being attacked by the enemy?

Answer. I think if we had left a rear guard of cavalry, we could have protected them and carried them out of all that. I think that by all means every man that could get a horse should have gone out There were 2,000 horses left there.

Question. Who had them?

Answer. They were artillery horses and captured horses I had captured a great many myself and left them there.

Question. You are mistaken about the number, I think

Answer I guess you will not find any officer there who will not say what I do I do not think there was less than 2,000. Of course, I guess at the number.

By the JUDGE-ADVOCATE:

Question. The horses were of no use whatever in the defense of the place?

Answer. No, sir.

By General WHITE

Question. How much force do you suppose the enemy had on the north side of the Potomac at that time?

Answer. From the best information I could get, they had about 7,000 men.

Question. I mean their entire force?

Answer. Do you mean over in Maryland?

R—4

Question. Yes, sir

Answer. About 135,000, I reckon.

Question And you, in passing out with the cavalry, turned the entire left flank of that force ?

Answer. We did not turn the flank at all. We were on one side of the mountain and their force was on the other   At that time there were none of them beyond Pleasant Valley, and we passed up on the southern side of the Blue Ridge, as we call it in Virginia, until we passed them.   They were in Maryland, though, but by going on as far as Chambersburg we got entirely around them.   Stuart took pretty much the same route, only he crossed the Potomac higher up, and came around a week ago and a little over.

Question Suppose the infantry had been started out at the time the cavalry started from Harper's Ferry, when they were passing up that road what would have prevented the force under Jackson in the valley from attacking our column ?

Answer. Jackson at that time was in Pleasant Valley.

Question You are mistaken in that ; he was in front of us at Bolivar Heights.

Answer. He had not crossed over the mountain

Question On Sunday night ?

Answer No, sir.

Question. We fought his troops on Sunday afternoon before you left

Answer I do not know where in the world he could have been.

Question. In passing up that road with the entire command, if the lines of the enemy were stretched around to the Potomac at Shepherdstown, would it not have been probable that they would have known of our departure and attacked us there ?

Answer. There is a probability of it ; but at night, that way, I do not think we would have had anything more than their pickets to have attended to.

Question. You think they would have allowed our entire command to have gone out without an attack ?

Answer. I think they would

Question Why ?

Answer. We had seen no indication of anything else when we went, nothing like showing fight in any force.

Question. That was because your passage up the river was pretty rapid?

Answer. That was so ; we were going along moderately fast.

Question. Did you go about 10 miles an hour?

Answer I think we went at least that I do not want it understood that I looked upon Colonel Miles as a traitor I never did I served under him too long. I think he was a loyal man.

By the COURT :

Question What is your opinion in regard to the capacity of Colonel Miles for that command?

Answer. I think he was entirely capable ten days before the surrender of Harper's Ferry.

Question. You made the remark a few minutes ago that in that conversation you discovered what was the matter. What was the matter with Colonel Miles?

Answer. That is a thing I did not care about telling, but as you have asked me I suppose I must I think he had taken too much to drink I never had seen it the case before, but that was my impression at the time. I had been serving under him before for three or four months, and I never saw that the case with him until that time ; therefore I paid no attention to what he said.

Question. Did he continue in that state during the remaining portion of your stay?

Answer. Yes, sir; that was the Thursday week before the evacuation of Harper's Ferry. That was the first I ever discovered in him anything of the kind.

By the JUDGE-ADVOCATE

Question How did his condition manifest itself ; was it in confusion of ideas?

Answer. Not at all.

Question. In excitement?

Answer. No, sir ; he seemed to be stubborn, nothing else. In the fix he was in then, he would not believe anything you would tell him.

By General WHITE :

Question Do you mean to be understood that during
the siege of Harper's Ferry Colonel Miles was not intox-
icated all the time, but he seemed to have enough to
make him stubborn ? Do you think he was drinking ?

Answer. I think he was.   I had been reporting to him
once or twice a week for at least two or three months,
and I had never found him anything else but perfectly
straightforward in every respect until about that time.

As Col Miles was dead, the court could not take any
action towards him, except that it was shown that he
acted with utter incapacity, which led to the shameful
surrender.

Col. Ford was dismissed from the service. Gen.
White was found to have acted with capacity and courage. Gen McClellan was mildly censured for not marching over 6 miles a day , and that he could and should
have rescued the garrison at Harper's Ferry

The affair may be briefly summed up as follows

Col Miles should not have vacated Maryland Heights,
and of course should not have surrendered, as by remaining there he could have held the place until the arrival
of Gen. McClellan

Col Miles was found guilty of drunkenness by a
prevous court of inquiry at the first battle of Bull Run.

In bidding adieu to this unfortunate affair, an extract
is given from a Southern historian, John Esten Cooke,
who served on the staff of Gen. R. E. Lee .

"Harper's Ferry had fallen—fallen at the moment
when McClellan was only a short march from it, with
almost nothing between ; at the moment when Miles
could almost hear the shouts of the troops coming to his
relief, when in a few hours McLaws on Maryland Heights
would have been captured , Jackson would have been
cut off from a junction with the main body, and Lee
would have been defeated—swallowed up in the Potomac like the Egyptians in the Red Sea."

A few days before the cavalry left Harper's Ferry four of the Rangers, Joseph T. Divine, D J. Harper, T. J. McCutcheon, and Charles White were doing special picket duty with the 87th Ohio regiment at Sandy Hook. As the enemy advanced on Harper's Ferry this squad became separated from the regiment and went out through Maryland and Pennsylvania, capturing three rebels on the way, and took them into York, Pa. These were the first "Johnnies" the citizens had seen, and, of course, they were a kind of curiosity. The Rangers were lionized for this heroic achievement and escorted to the hotel, where an ovation was given them, and a grand dinner which the boys enjoyed

We will now turn to Gen McClellan's army that came up from Washington in pursuit of Gen Lee's army and to give it battle The Union army arrived at Frederick, Md., September 12, and came into possession of the general order of Gen. Lee previously referred to

When McClellan learned the plans of the Confederate commander he set his army in motion to thwart them.

He ordered Gen Franklin's corps to pass through Crampton's Gap and relieve Harper's Ferry The corps of Reno and Hooker, under command of Gen Burnside, were to move through Turner's Gap. These movements were executed rather slowly. They arrived at the Gap September 14, and were within 7 miles of Harper's Ferry when it surrendered "So near and yet so far !" Gen. Lee had recalled Longstreet and Hill from Boonsboro and Hagerstown to check the advance of McClellan and had taken position behind trees and ledges of rocks on South Mountain As the Union troops advanced they were met by a terrific fire from the enemy, who was entirely concealed from view This Indian mode of fighting continued all day, the Union troops gaining step by step, until about 6 o'clock a final charge carried the slopes of the mountain, completely routing the enemy and capturing nearly two regiments.

This engagement, fought September 14, is known in history as the " Battle of South Mountain," and should not be confounded with Antietam, as it often is.

The Union troops lost in killed and wounded over 2,000, Gen Reno, of the Ninth corps, being killed Among the wounded was Lieut. Col. Rutherford B Hayes, of the 23d Ohio, who did good service there, and did good service in after years as President of the United States The enemy lost in killed and wounded 1,920, and 200 prisoners, one cannon, and three battle flags—General Garland being among the killed. The Union troops fought with sublime bravery, having great obstacles to surmount, climbing a steep mountain and driving the enemy from behind trees, rocks, and stone fences, where they were strongly posted, and at nightfall rested on the summit of South Mountain.

The next morning, September 15, the Union army pressed forward through the passes into the valley of the Antietam, where the enemy was found strongly posted on a high and commanding position The day was largely consumed by Gen McClellan in reconnoitering for position That night he learned of the capitulation of Harper's Ferry.

This same enemy that was now in his front had a few weeks previously baffled and driven him from the Peninsula It had also defeated Gen. Pope on the plains of Manassas, and had compelled the surrender of Harper's Ferry. The question had been asked in great seriousness " could this army be defeated ?" It had now been on Maryland soil eight days Thus far it had avoided a practical test of strength with its adversary ; that issue could not be deferred any longer; a great battle must be fought to settle that question The battle of South Mountain had been a victory for Gen. McClellan ;

it was also a victory for Gen Lee, as it enabled him to hold the Union army back two days, thereby enabling his own army to be reunited, and it was now ready to settle the question wether it could remain on Northern soil or whether it would be compelled to seek refuge in the land of its conception

September 16 found Gen. Lee's army in position on the west bank of Antietam Creek, his left resting on the Potomac, and right on the creek, facing east. The stream was crossed by four bridges and a ford, all except the northernmost being strongly guarded Gen McClellan's plan of action was to cross at the upper or north bridge, attack the enemy's left wing with vigor, and while this was in progress force the passages of the lower bridges, and attack the enemy's right. There was perhaps no especial strategy in this plan, in fact, it was about the only course to follow, since the enemy had choice of position and was of necessity on the defensive There had been considerable cannonading during the day, and if there was any advantage resulting from it, it was in favor of the Union position, owing, perhaps, to the superiority of guns. Late in the evening, Gen Hooker crossed at the upper ford, and with Gen Meade's division attacked the Confederate left. Owing to the early approach of darkness little was accomplished, both belligerents resting on their arms for the night

Early on the morning of September 17 Gen. Hooker opened an attack on Jackson's corps, which was forced back in great disorder, losing two guns and about 800 prisoners ; while Hooker advanced his lines to hold the position thus obtained a little too far and was attacked on both flanks with great vigor by fresh troops, and was in turn compelled to retire. Gen. Mansfield's corps that crossed the stream during the night was ordered to the relief of Hooker Mansfield's troops had just gone into position when that commander was mortally wounded (he died the next day), a few moments later Gen. Hooker was borne from the field, seriously wounded.

Gen. Sumner's corps that crossed at early morning came up with fresh troops and drove back the enemy beyond the Dunkard church, capturing nearly 2,000 prisoners and five guns and several battle flags. The enemy sent fresh troops from their right, consisting of McLaw's and Walker's corps which had just arrived from Harper's Ferry, and threw Sumner's troops into some confusion, compelling them to relinquish the ground around to the Dunkard church. About 12 o'clock Gen. Franklin arrived from Crampton's Pass, just in time to check the advance of more fresh troops sent over from the Confederate right.

While this mode of seesaw fighting continued the entire forenoon and was exceedingly stubborn and disastrous on the Federal right, the left and center remained quiet as uninterested spectators.

BURNSIDE'S BRIDGE AT ANTIETAM CREEK.

Gen. Burnside had been ordered at 8 o'clock to bring forward the center and left and force a passage of the bridges in his front and attack the enemy's right. By

some misunderstanding of orders that movement was
not executed until 2 o'clock.   By 3 o'clock the ridges in
front of Sharpsburg were carried, capturing a rebel battery   At this juncture there appeared the last of Lee's
army from Harper's Ferry (A. P. Hill's corps).   These
fresh troops and other reinforcements from the enemy's
left fell upon Burnside's force and drove them from
the crest of the hill, retaking the battery   As operations
under Hooker had ceased on the right, this was practically the end of one of the most hotly contested and
bloody battles of the war, and probably the most disastrous to both sides, considering the time occupied and
numbers engaged

Every man of Gen. Lee's forces had been actively
engaged, while Gen. McClellan had 35,000 men in sight
of the battlefield all day that were idle spectators.

The enemy's forces ought to and could have been an-
nihilated, or captured.   It was not because Lee, with
his army divided for three days in presence of his enemy,
had not invited destruction, nor because the 70,000 acting in concert could not have overwhelmed the 40,000 ,
nor was it for lack of courage of men, or arms, or opportunity, but because the attack had been made by regimental front, disjointed and unsupported, instead of
heavy column and both wings simultaneously.   By the
latter method McClellan, with troops at hand, could have
prevented the enemy from reinforcing at any point

On both sides the troops fought with a courageous
bravery and determination that baffles description.   It
is doubtful if it was surpassed by any battle of the war.

A few illustrations of regimental and brigade losses
will show the unparalleled severity of the fighting

One company of recruits of the 12th Massachusetts
went in with 72 men—but two escaped unhurt.   The
16th Connecticut, also recruits, went in with 940 men—
lost 432   On the Confederate side Drayton's Brigade,
with 1,150 men, lost 554, including five out of six of their

regimental commanders , while Hood's Brigade lost 325 out of 550, including every regimental and staff officer. The Confederates lost three generals killed and eight wounded, while Gen McClellan lost two generals, Mansfield and Richardson, killed, and six wounded.

Gen. McClellan reported his losses at—killed, 2,010 ; wounded, 9,500 ; missing, 1,043—total, 12,553.

The Confederate reports are fragmentary. The best authorities place their losses from 20,000 to 25,000, including over 7,000 prisoners. Gen. McClellan reports the burying of 2,700 of the enemy's dead.

As already stated, Antietam was the bloodiest battle of the war of the rebellion. More men were killed on that one day than on any other one day of the war. There were battles with greater loss of life, but they were not fought out in one day as at Antietam. At Gettysburg, Chancellorsville, and Spottsylvania, the fighting covered three days or more ; at the Wilderness, Cold Harbor, Shiloh, Stone River, Chickamauga, and Atlanta, the losses were divided between two days of fighting ; but at Antietam the bloody work commenced at sunrise and by 4 o'clock that afternoon it was over. A table showing the losses in the principal engagements of the war presents these facts more definitely.

	Date	Killed	Wounded.	Missing .	Aggregate.
Antietam.	Sept 17. 1862 .	2 108	9 549	753	12 410
Gettysburg	July 1–3, 1863	3,070	14,497	5,434	23,001
Spottsylvania	May 8–18, 1864 .	2,725	13 416	2 258	18,399
Wilderness	May 5–7, 1864	2,246	12,037	3 383	17,666
Chancellorsville	May 1–3, 1863. .	1,606	9,762	5,919	17,287
Chickamauga	Sept 19–20, 1863	1,656	9,749	4,774	16 179
Cold Harbor	June 1–4, 1864	1,844	9,077	1,816	12 737
Fredericksburg	Dec. 11–14, 1863	1,284	9,600	1,769	12,653
Manassas.	Aug 28–30, 1862	1,747	8,452	4,263	14,462
Shiloh	April 6–7, 1862 .	1,754	8,408	2 885	13,047
Stone River	Dec 31,1862, Jan 2,1863	1,730	7,802	3 717	13,249
Petersburg .	June 15–19, 1864	1,688	8,513	1,185	11,386
Atlanta including Peach Tree and Ezra Church and the battle of July, 22	July 1–31. 1864	1,110	5,915	2,694	9,719
Chattanooga	Nov 23–25, 1863.	687	4,346	349	5 382

The percentage of loss on the Union side was over 15 per cent of the entire strength of the Army and fully 20 per cent of the troops under fire. Many brigades lost one-third to one-half the men taken into action, and twelve regiments lost more than 50 per cent., the 12th Massachusetts heading the list with 67 per cent., while the lowest of the twelve, the 14th Indiana, lost 56 per cent.

Wellington lost 12 per cent. at Waterloo ; Napoleon 14½ per cent. at Austerlitz and 14 per cent. at Marengo The average losses of both armies at Magenta and Solferino, in 1859, was less than 9 per cent. At Koniggràtz, in 1866, it was 6 per cent At Wörth, Mars-la-Tour, Gravelotte, and Sedan, in 1870, the average loss was 12 per cent.

The marvel of German fighting in the Franco-Prussian war was by the Third Westphalian Infantry at Mars-la-Tour. It took 3,000 men into action and lost 40 4 per cent. Next to this record was that of the Garde-Schützen battalion, 1,000 strong, at Metz, which lost 46 1 per cent.

As striking as are these figures on the Union side they are equalled if not exceeded by those of the Confederates. It is impossible to give the figures with entire accuracy, for in making up their returns they included the losses at Harper's Ferry, South Mountain, and Antietam, aggregating 1,886 killed, 9,348 wounded, and 1,377 missing, a sum total of 12,601, or, according to Gen. Lee's report, over 20 per cent. of the troops which he took into Maryland, and the greater part of which loss was sustained at Antietam.

The terrific nature of the contest sustained by them may be judged from the fact that many brigades lost one-half the men engaged, and in three at least this proportion was exceeded. Out of 42 Confederate regiments given as sustaining a loss in any one battle during the entire war of over 50 per cent., ten made this record in one day at Antietam, headed by the First Texas, of Hood's division, which lost 82.3 per cent., the highest recorded for the war.

These figures on both sides attest the bravery and obstinacy with which the opposing lines in open field, without breastworks of any kind, stood and tore each other to shreds.

GEN. McCLELLAN.

The political questions which were involved in the contest ought not, under ordinary circumstances, to enter into consideration ; but Antietam forms an exception, for upon the result on that field depended the greatest political stroke of modern times, the promulgation of the policy of emancipation by the President of the United States. When the summer of 1862 brought disaster after disaster to the Union cause, finally culminating in the invasion of Maryland by Gen. Lee, Abraham

Lincoln determined on the emancipation of the slaves. "I made," said Mr. Lincoln, "a solemn vow before God that if Gen. Lee was driven back from Maryland I would crown the result by the declaration of freedom to the slaves."

Gen. Lee was driven from Maryland, and on September 22, 1862, President Lincoln issued the proclamation

Gen. McClellan, unquestionably, should have renewed the attack on the morning of the 18th. That day both commanders agreed to eight hours' armistice to bury the dead and care for the wounded. Instead of burying his dead Gen. Lee's army was engaged cutting trenches through the Chesapeake and Ohio Canal, and that night crossed the Potomac into Virginia, leaving their dead unburied and wounded uncared for. If the reader will consult history he will find this is not the first time Gen. Lee violated a pledge of honor.

The Confederate campaign in Maryland had ended. It lasted just two weeks. Inaugurated as a triumphant invasion, with flying colors, it ended in a skedaddle between two days, with their meagre supply of "Liberty and Protection " entirely exhausted.

While this battle was in progress the cavalry did valuable service guarding the flanks and doing scouting duty, capturing nearly 2,000 prisoners from the enemy's army, in which the Loudoun Rangers bore a conspicuous part.

The company was now put to active duty, bearing dispatches and scouting for the army while it lay along the Potomac from Monocacy to Shepherdstown. The last of October Gen. McClellan began to cross the Potomac at Brunswick, the Rangers acting as guides. November 1st we encamped at Waterford, where the army rested for two days. W. S. Keyes joined the company here, the first recruit we had since the Waterford fight. We continued as guides until the Army of the

Potomac went into winter quarters on the Rappahannock, when the Rangers were ordered back to the Eighth
Corps, which lay along the Potomac. Our camp was
established at Point of Rocks, in the old warehouse between the Chesapeake and Ohio Canal and the river.
Those who were captured and paroled at Waterford were
now exchanged and returned to duty, Lieut. Slater returned, carrying his arm in a sling, and being unfit for
field duty he was appointed Provost Marshal of Point of
Rocks His extensive acquaintance enabled him to
decide who was entitled to take goods through the
blockade.

CHAPTER VI.

CAMPED AT POINT OF ROCKS—MOVED TO BERLIN—LIEUT SLATER
    RESIGNED ON ACCOUNT OF WOUNDS—CAMP MOVED TO BOLIVAR
    HEIGHTS—TO BERRYVILLE—CONFEDERATE ARMY MARCHES
    NORTHWARD

It was evident to all who saw Lieut Slater that he
would never be fit for active duty, which would make
the place of 1st lieutenant vacant. The question of his
successor had been mentioned around camp   Charles
A. Webster was ambitious and wanted the place, and
perhaps it is but fair to state if it had been left to the
company he would have been chosen On one occasion, when Capt. Means was absent, Webster took the
bull by the horns (as was his method of doing things)
and concluded to hold an election for 1st lieutenant
He called the company in line and declared the office
vacant, and announced his candidacy, and concluded by
saying, "All in favor of Webster for 1st lieutenant step
two paces to the front," when nearly the entire company stepped to the front, he declared himself elected
1st lieutenant.   Such an election was without prece-

dent, and was, of course, revolutionary in the extreme. On Capt. Means' return he was furious, and declared the election a usurpation of both military and civil rights Means never liked Webster, and had been endeavoring to get rid of him in a quiet way, but he was no longer very quiet about it. Webster's connection with the company ceased late in November.

While encamped in the warehouse Albert C. Hawk, Robert Zee, James Monegan, Peter C Fry, John McDevitt, Charles Pekam, John Lenhart, Phillip H. Heater, James Daily, J. N. Johnson and Jacob Dixon joined the company. Early in December the camp was moved to the old Catoctin Furnace across the river in Loudoun.

In December a small squad of the company went on a raid to Waterford, where White's command was encountered again. As our number was so small we fell back toward Lovettsville We captured one prisoner, Ned Moreland, and lost two, W S. Keyes and McMullen, the latter being wounded—Lieut Keyes was slighty wounded in the arm. The prisoner we captured took the oath of allegiance to the United States, and served the Rangers efficiently and faithfully to the close of the war "as chief cook." The camp was changed to Heater's Island, in the Potomac River, about the 15th of December, where we enjoyed our first grand treat of the war ; we got paid off in brand new greenbacks The most of the boys got six months' pay.

The last of December the camp was moved back to Point of Rocks, in the old warehouse The latter part of January, 1863, a portion of the 13th Pennsylvania Cavalry, in command of Maj. Byrne, and the Rangers started on a raid in Virginia ; the first stop was made at Umbaugh's still-house where the entire command formed in line. George Umbaugh, with bucket and cup, went from man to man and quenched the thirst of all with good, fresh apple brandy The column moved

on, arriving at Leesburg about 10 o'clock a. m., charging in King street   The porch of the old Picket Hotel,
where is now located the palatial Leesburg Inn, was full
of rebels, who ran through the house and out the back
way.   The company dismounted, entering through the
hall to the back yard, but all had disappeared   Fresh
tracks were noticed leading to a small stable, which was
entered by a lieutenant of the 13th Pennsylvania Cavalry and one of the young Rangers, both climbing up
into the hay loft.   The lieutenant ordered the Ranger
to draw his sabre and thrust it down through the hay.
On giving this order the hay began to quiver, and
showed unmistakable signs of being inhabited.   At the
first thrust the forms of two rebels sprung from under
the hay at the other end of the loft   They proved to
be two of White's men, Charles Cooper and John Tay-
lor.   The first thing they discovered was two revolvers
leveled on them, with the demand to "surrender."
The request was meekly complied with   The rest of
the Johnnies did not risk a hay mow, and made good
their escape.   The command moved on through Waterford and Hillsboro back *via* Harper's Ferry and down
the tow path to Point of Rocks

The 1st of February the company moved to Brunswick and encamped upon the hill near the old cemetery,
going into winter quarters.   Gen. Hancock's Second
Corps was encamped here in the fall, and had cut timber and erected excellent winter quarters, but had
moved away about the time they were finished.   We
readily transformed them into quarters for the Rangers.

Our first recruit here was Thos. W. Agan, who was
immediately appointed "horse farrier."   Webster gives
the definition as "horse doctor"   The dictionary is
wrong or else the Rangers were most outrageously
deceived in this appointment   Tom was a first-class
fellow, but probably knew less about a horse than any

Capt. Daniel M. Keyes, Co. A.

Sergt. Joseph T. Divine, Co. A.

other man in the company On one occasion a horse
got loose and wallowed in yellow mud. That evening
as we went to feed, Agan wanted to know where that
new dun horse came from Aside from the horse Tom
was well posted, particularly on politics

A sad and irreparable loss now befel the Rangers,
Lieut L W. Slater was finally discharged February 19,
1863, on account of his wounds. He was not only
obeyed and respected, but loved by all , a large, physically well-built man, a true type of American soldier,
and as brave as a lion.

Lieut Keyes was promoted to 1st lieutenant. Instead
of promoting the Orderly Sergeant or any other sergeant to be 2d lieutenant, the saddler was elected 2d lieutenant. On the morning of February 20 Capt. Means
formed the company in line, back of his tent, in a deep
snow, for the purpose of electing a 2d lieutenant. All
those who were in favor of E. R. Gover for second lieutenant were asked to step two paces to the front, when
a few more than a majority stepped out All who
favored Orderly Sergeant James A. Cox for second lieutenant were asked to step two paces to the front, when
the remainder stepped out A majority having voted
for Gover, he was declared elected The boys dubbed
him "Four Eyes." He was a kind and pleasant officer,
but perhaps a little old and slow for the position The
following recruits were mustered here : Thos. W. Agan,
John Ambrose, Joseph Bagent, Wm Bull, Edward Bond,
George P. and Presley A. Davis, Peter Dorherty, W. H
Hoover, Michael Ryan, and Edward Snyder.

Geo. W. Hough died in camp, of fever. We took him
to Waterford and buried him with the honors of war

Paymaster-Major Brigham gave us a very pleasant
call March 1, and left with us four months' pay. Everybody enjoyed the call, especially those to whom we were
indebted.

R—5

About February 20, Sergt F. B. Anderson got a leave of absence to go to Taylortown, Va., to attend a ball, in which he and his sister, Miss Mollie, were to take a prominent part. The ball was held at the residence of James Filler While on the floor dancing, about 11 o'clock p m, Lieut. Marlow and squad of White's Confederate cavalry entered the ball room, and with about a dozen revolvers pointing in Sergt. Anderson's face, demanded a surrender, which was very reluctantly complied with, but the next step, a trip to Richmond, was still harder, as it would last much longer His sister, Miss Mollie, came to the rescue. She threw her arms around Marlow's neck, weeping bitterly, pleading only as woman can plead, to spare her brother a trip to Libby, which was almost sure death. Marlow wilted He told her if she would dance " the next set " with him he would parole her brother. She gladly consented What came so near being a tragedy was now suddenly turned into a comedy. The Johnnies took partners, Sergt. Anderson took the violin and played "The girl I left behind me " Lieut Marlow and Miss Mollie led off, " Balance to your partners,"—" Ladies to the right,"—" Promenade all " It was hard to tell who was the hero of the evening. When the set ended Marlow and his men departed, taking Mr. Stout Williams with them to Richmond as a witness in the Webster case, which we shall speak of later Sergt Anderson went to Point of Rocks next day, and was sent from there to Camp Parole, at Annapolis, Md , remaining until exchanged

The first of March the company moved to Bolivar Heights—early in the month while the company was raiding in Virginia—and on their return about twelve of the boys left the column to call on some lady friends, and in consequence did not reach camp until the next day. For this offense of leaving the command without

leave, and in the enemy's country, Capt. Means declared
them worthy of severe punishment, and had them arrested and put in the lockup. This was the boys' first
experience behind the bars and was somewhat humiliating. After remaining there several hours Capt. Means
informed them that this being their first offense he
would release them, and gave them a severe lecture on
military discipline.

While a portion of the company was returning from
a raid in Loudoun, and when between Waterford and
Lovettsville, Sergt. James H. Corbin was shot from
ambush and killed, about 10 o'clock at night. This
was a sad loss, as Sergt. Corbin was a most excellent
soldier, and one of the first to cast his fortune with the
Rangers.

The last of March the company, with three companies of the 14th Pennsylvania Cavalry, in command
of Maj. Daily, were on an extended raid in the direction
of Snicker's Gap. When west of Purcellville a still-
house in operation was passed, and quite a number of
the Pennsylvanians stopped and filled their canteens
and drank freely, while the whisky was yet warm,
being only a few hours old, and it soon took effect It
was with difficulty the command was gotten back to
camp safely.

April 18, 1863, Jacob E Boryer was discharged on
account of wounds received at Leesburg.

The last of the month the company moved to Berryville, in the Shenandoah Valley, and was actively engaged in scouting and carrying dispatches to Winchester. There had been considerabla complaint about
Commissary-Sergeant William S. Keyes being absent
and not providing the men with rations These com-
plaints had become so loud that Capt. Means was forced
to recognize them, and at roll call ordered an election.
Everybody yelled "Milt. Gregg," and that gentleman

was declared elected. This was especially complimentary to Gregg, as it was the first and last time the
company was called upon to choose its non-commissioned
officers It was a popular selection Gregg always
provided the boys with something to eat, and occasionally something to drink, if nothing more than black
coffee

A few days after our arrival at Berryville the writer
had his leg broken by his horse falling. The Rangers
not being provided with a doctor, an ambulance of the
67th Pennsylvania Infantry was sent for and the patient
taken to the hospital of that regiment, where the
broken bones were skilfully set and the patient tenderly
cared for

April 22, Capt. Means, with twenty of the Rangers,
accompanied by Lieut Wykoff, 1st New York Cavalry,
and Lieut. Powell, with forty men of the 12th West
Virginia Infantry, crossed the Shenandoah River at
Snicker's Ferry, and attacked a camp of Confederate
cavalry, capturing Capt. Leopold and six men, and took
them to Winchester

May 6 Maj. Thayer, Paymaster, came up from Harper's
Ferry to pay the troops stationed at Berryville Dan
Harper was sent to Winchester with dispatches to Gen.
Milroy to have his troops in readiness to receive their
pay. The next day the Rangers escorted Maj. Thayer
to Winchester, staying all night and returning the next
day

We had two recruits while camping at Berryville;
Richard Virts and George Wilt, two loyal citizens of
Loudoun, then cast their fortunes with the boys

The Army of the Potomac had changed commanders
twice since the battle of Antietam.

Gen. McClellan had so completely exhausted the
patience of the Nation by his campaigns of " masterly
inactivity " that the President felt compelled to relieve

him of the command, and on November 7 appointed Gen. Ambrose E. Burnside as his successor.

In West Point theory McClellan was well equipped for a great general, but when he confronted the enemy on the field of combat he lacked confidence in his own ability. He also lacked aggressiveness, which was in so much demand during the Civil War.

Gen. Burnside was also a graduate of West Point, and had made a good reputation as a corps commander. He fought the great battle of Fredericksburg, but was defeated. His career as commander of the Army of the Potomac was too brief to be fairly judged. At his own request he was relieved.

GEN. BURNSIDE.

With the Ninth Corps he was transferred to the Army of the Cumberland, and in the East Tennessee campaign he made a brilliant reputation as an able commander, a successful fighter, and a strategist of the highest order.

January 25, 1863, Gen Joseph Hooker was appointed
Commander-in-Chief of the Army of the Potomac   He
had commanded a corps in the Army of the Potomac
from the beginning, and was popular, and earned the
title of " Fighting Joe Hooker."   He was a fine looking
officer, and he knew it.   Perhaps he was a little too
much inclined to vanity.   In his annunciamento he
characterized his army as the " finest army on the
planet."

President Lincoln accompanied the appointment with
a private letter to Gen. Hooker, which illustrates the
peculiar genius and practical life of the great President
He wrote :

"I have placed you at the head of the Army of the
Potomac , Of course I have done this on what appears
to me sufficient reason, and yet I think it best for you
to know there are some things in regard to which I am
not quite satisfied with you.   I believe you to be a brave
and skillful soldier, which, of course, I like.   I also believe you do not mix politics with your profession, in
which you are right.   You have confidence in yourself,
which is a valuable, if not indispensable, quality.   You
are ambitious, which within reasonable bounds does
good rather than harm, but I think that during Gen.
Burnside's command of the army you have taken coun-
sel of your ambition, and thwarted him as much as you
could, in which you did a great wrong to the country
and to a most meritorious and honorable brother officer.
I have heard in such a way as to believe it, of your recently saying that both the Army and the Government
needed a dictator   Of course it was not for this, but in
spite of it, that I have given you the command.   Only
those generals who gain successes can set up dictators.
What I now ask of you is military success, and I will
risk the dictatorship.   The Government will support
you to the utmost of its ability, which is neither more
nor less than it has done and will do for all commanders.
I much fear that the spirit which you have aided to in-
fuse into the Army, of criticising their commander, and
withholding confidence from him, will now turn upon

you. I shall assist you as far as I can to put it down. Neither you nor Napoleon, were he alive again, could get any good out of any army while such a spirit prevails in it ; and now beware of rashness, but with energy and sleepless vigilance go forward and give us victories.''

GEN. HOOKER.

Gen. Hooker fought the bloody battle of Chancellorsville, where he was severely wounded and defeated. After the battle of Chancellorsville, a village of but one house, the Confederate army felt sufficiently elated to attempt a second invasion of the North. The rebel cavalry attacked our pickets at Winchester May 19. Gen. Milroy made short work of this raid, driving the Confederates south of Mount Jackson. All was quiet for about two weeks. June 6 Rosser, with his Confederate cavalry, attacked our pickets at Berryville, but was driven south of the Shenandoah River, with a loss of about twenty. The first brigade of the Eighth Corps, Gen. McReynolds commanding, was now concentrated at Berryville. June 12, at 4 p. m., Gen. Ewell's Confederate Corps attacked Gen. McReynolds sharply, the fighting lasting until dark, Gen. McReynolds losing about forty killed and two hundred wounded. That night our forces formed a junction with Gen. Milroy at Winchester. The next day, June 13, Ewell attacked Milroy with great fury, the latter being behind fortifications, the rebels were slaughtered, losing over two hundred killed. The Confederates threw shells into the fort at intervals during the night, perhaps not enough to make it very dangerous, but just enough to keep those on the inside on the tip-toe of expectation; this cannonading was kept up at intervals during the entire day of the 14th. During the night Gen. Milroy evacuated the fort and took up a position east of Winchester, to keep communication open with Harper's Ferry. Ewell attacked our forces fiercely on the morning of the 15th with infantry and artillery in large numbers, gradually forcing Milroy to fall back to Harper's Ferry. In this last engagement Milroy lost between three and four hundred killed and about twelve hundred prisoners, including Alexander's Baltimore Battery; the prisoners lost were mostly wounded. The Union army, though defeated, made a heroic fight. Milroy had about seven thousand troops at Winchester, while the enemy had near twenty thousand. The Union forces under Gen. French concentrated on Maryland Heights. It will be remembered that this army that defeated Milroy at Winchester was what historians have been pleased to term the flower of the Confederacy, on their way to Gettysburg, where the rays of the July sun severely scorched that Southern posy.

For the last few weeks the Rangers had not remained long enough at any one place to call it a camp, although the camp equipage was between Weverton and Brunswick, while a portion of the company was at Harper's Ferry.

Gen. French, in command of the latter place, ordered Capt. Means to send three reliable and cool-headed men into Virginia, east of the Blue Ridge, as scouts to locate and ascertain if possible the strength and movements of the enemy, who were supposed to be on the eve of crossing the Potomac into Maryland. Sergt. Jas. H. Beatty, Joseph T. Ritchie and Commissary Sergt. Milton S Gregg were selected. They crossed the Potomac above Brunswick Ferry, going south in the direction of Snickersville, where they obtained valuable information, returning through Loudoun. When near Waterford they learned that five rebels were in town. They took advantage of the situation ; charging into town, they completely routed those five rebels, who proved to be White's men, and captured one by the name of Leslie, and two horses, taking them into Harper's Ferry, arriving about 11 o'clock at night.

The writer, who had his leg broken at Berryville and had been taken to the hospital, returned to the company while at Harper's Ferry and reported for duty. It was reported the rebels were crossing the Potomac into Maryland, near Noland's Ferry, and the Rangers were ordered to ascertain the correctness of the report. The command went down the river as far as Monocacy, but were not able to learn of any troops crossing near there. That night the company forded the river to Heater's Island to obtain forage for the horses Capt. Means ordered the men to lie down and take a little rest while the horses were eating. As we had been almost constantly in the saddle for several days, everybody was sound asleep directly. About twelve o'clock Zack Robison, Capt Means' servant, aroused the men and told them a squad of men were leaving the island, going towards the Virginia shore with horses Our men rushed to their horses, but to their consternation and surprise found quite a number missing All that could

be mounted started in pursuit   About a mile from the
river, on the Virginia side, we struck a body of rebel
cavalry, and charged and scattered them in every direction in the darkness, recapturing all our horses and
several more, and severely wounding one man, shooting
him through the body.   We returned to the Maryland side about daylight and camped in the edge of
the mountain, north of Point of Rocks.   That evening our teamster, Geo H. Divine, arrived from above
Brunswick with camp equipage.   Some of the men
had gone to the Point of Rocks, some were preparing supper, while others were taking a much needed
sleep ; while in this condition our camp was attacked
about sundown, the enemy capturing thirteen of our
boys and wounding John W. Virts, who was shot
through the breast.   The enemy proved to be Col
White's Confederate cavalry, who crossed the Potomac
River at Grubb's Ford, below Brunswick, June 17
Company B, Lieut. Crown commanding, was sent across
the country to attack our camp from the north, while
Col. White, with Companies A. C, D, E, and F, marched
down the tow-path and attacked from the south   The
successful achievement of White and Crown on this
occasion is attributed to the fact that their advance
guards wore Federal uniforms, and were taken for our
own men.

John W. Virts, who was severely wounded and taken
prisoner, had formerly belonged to the rebel army,
was a member of the Loudoun Artillery, and wounded
at the first battle of Bull Run, who, when he was able
to be moved, was sent home to recuperate, and who,
when he recovered, instead of rejoining his battery,
bade adieu to the Confederacy and went to Maryland
and took the oath of allegiance to the Government of
the United States   Afterwards he joined our company
When taken prisoner some of White's men who had

been his former neighbors, and evidently possessed of a devil, instead of trying to comfort a wounded soldier, though an enemy, whose life's blood was apparently slowly but surely ebbing away, did all they could to make his short stay on this earth miserable by preferring charges against him for alleged desertion, and tried to have him executed One of Milroy's men taken at Winchester a few days previous, who belonged to an Ohio regiment, changed uniforms with him, which to some extent disguised him. When taken to Richmond he gave his name as Jim Davis, and claimed to belong to an Ohio regiment, and adopted that name. While there, on Belle Island, the rebel officer, Sergt. Haight, tried to find him by pretending to have a letter from friends at home, but the scheme would not work, and Jack Virts was finally exchanged as Jim Davis Although he lived until the war was over, yet his wounds carried him to an untimely grave

The 18th of June the Rangers moved to Harper's Ferry, and soon afterwards to Frederick, Md., where they were assigned to active duty scouting and bearing dispatches for the Eighth Corps, at that time in command of Gen. Schenck

CHAPTER VII

THE GETTYSBURG CAMPAIGN—FREDERICK—ELLICOTT'S MILLS— RELAY HOUSE — TENNALLYTOWN — CAMPED AT DRIPPING SPRINGS—THE FIGHT AT GRAY'S FARM

June 22 the Confederate army crossed the Potomac at Shepherdstown and Williamsport, and marched direct to Pennsylvania. By the 28th that army was in possession of Chambersburg, York, and Carlisle, Pa., and threatening Harrisburg, Philadelphia, and, perhaps, New York.

Gen. Hookers' Army of the Potomac crossed the river at Edwards' Ferry the 25th and 26th of June, and concentrated at Frederick, Md.   Owing to some slight disagreement between himself and Gen. Halleck, Gen. Hooker tendered his resignation as Commander of the Army of the Potomac June 27, and it was immediately accepted, and the next morning Gen. George G. Meade was appointed as his successor.   The army, under Hooker, had been unsuccessful, and that this change proved to be the right thing at the right time all careful readers will admit.

GEN. MEADE.

Gen. Meade was a graduate of West Point, had served in the Mexican War, and had been in the Army of the Potomac since its organization ; commanded a corps under McClellan, Burnside, and Hooker, and, of course, brought valuable experience to his new position.   He wisely omitted the usual sky-scraping announcement,

and went to work in a familiar and business-like way.
The day after his appointment the army was in motion.
The cavalry, under Gen. Pleasanton, was hurried forward to engage and delay the enemy until the whole
army could come up The enemy was encountered by
Gen Buford June 29 near Gettysburg, but the vigorous
attack by Gen Reynolds with the First Corps July 1 at
Gettysburg settled the question as to the place where
the great battle was to be fought

When Gen Lee invaded the North for the second
time and marched into Pennsylvania, Gov Curtin called
out the militia to assist in repelling the intruder Lieut
L. W. Slater, who was discharged from the Rangers on
account of wounds three months before, and who was
living in Gettysburg, having attended school there, was
one among the first to respond. The wounds he received at Waterford were still unhealed, yet, with arm
in sling, he, with his regiment, the 26th Pennsylvania
V M., Col. Jennings commanding, arrived at Gettysburg at 9 a m on Friday, June 26, 1863, and was ordered to advance west of the town, on the Chambersburg pike, for the purpose of holding the enemy in
check. Against this order Col Jennings earnestly protested, as his command was composed largely of men
who had never before been in service, Company A
being made up of students from Pennsylvania College,
and the position was a very exposed one. However, he
took up the indicated position and posted his pickets.

Early in the afternoon the rebels appeared in force
and captured the pickets, about 40 in number. Col.
Jennings, who had on former occasions proven himself
a skillful officer, as cool as he was brave, saw the danger
of the position and divided his command into several
detachments, in order to make as formidable showing as
possible. The manœuver was successful, in that the
enemy did not risk a direct attack upon the regiment,

but contented himself with following at a more respect-
ful distance and firing an occasional volley, except at
Hunterstown, where the regiment made a decided stand.
It was here that Corpl. D. H. Yount, in the middle of
the road, just in front of the enemy, working with might
and main to bring his wet gun into action, was heard to
say "Oh, bless the gun, it will not go off."

The regiment was forced to again retreat, with a
further loss of 120 men. The pursuit was continued
until the regiment arrived at Harrisburg on the morning of Sunday, June 28, after having marched 54 out
of 60 continuous hours. Too much credit can not be
given Col Jennings for this masterly retreat and the
saving of his command from annihilation, for if the
rebels had known it was only one militia regiment
opposing them such a fate would have overtaken the
gallant Twenty-sixth

A bronze monument has since been erected at the
head of Chambersburg Street to commemorate the fact
that this regiment made the first opposition to the rebel
army occupying the town of Gettysburg.

Nearly at the very beginning of the battle Gen Reynolds fell a victim to his own gallantry and bravery.

As was his custom during an engagement, he rode, as
on this occasion, at the head of his troops, urging and
encouraging them to press forward, when he was shot
by a rebel sharpshooter, and died shortly afterward.

After the fall of Gen Reynolds the command devolved
upon Gen Doubleday until the arrival of Gen Howard
with the Eleventh Corps.

Two divisions of this corps went into action at once,
while the remaining division, through the forethought
and wise generalship of Gen. Howard, was ordered to
occupy Cemetery Hill, on the south of the town, which
provided for the contingency that occurred only three
hours later. Some time before it became apparent to

the ordinary observer that the Union forces would be
compelled to retreat before the superior number of the
rebels, Gen Howard had the heavy artillery removed
to Cemetery Hill, where, with the support of the
division of the Eleventh Corps, it furnished sufficient
re-enforcement to enable the Union forces to check the
further advance of the rebel army   During the night
additional troops arrived, and in the early morning of
July 2, Gen Meade, arriving, approved of the position
selected by Gen Howard the evening before, and made
the best possible disposition of his forces to meet the
rebel manœuvers of that day

July 2d opened clear and bright   Gen Lee attacked
the Union right, but soon the entire line was fiercely
engaged. It was blow for blow   The fighting was
exceedingly stubborn during the entire day, the night
closing the combat with the advantages favoring the
Union army.   During the night Gen. Lee placed his
artillery in position for an onslaught the next day,
which he felt sure would be final.   Gen Meade, in coun-
seling his commanders that night, insisted that that
was the time, and that was the place the final test should
be made, and he believed the morrow would decide

July 3d opened clear and hot.   Gen Meade lost no
time in attacking the enemy early, and succeeded in
forcing back part of their lines   The rebels did not
renew the battle, and suddenly everything became as
quiet as a graveyard, which lasted until about 1 o'clock
when there suddenly began one of the greatest artillery
duels ever known in the history of battles.

The enemy opened with about 125 guns from Semi-
nary Ridge, which was replied to by 80 (all there was
room for) from Cemetery Ridge.   This cannonading
was continued for about two hours, when Gen. Hunt,
Meade's Chief of Artillery, ordered his guns to cease
firing, partly to cool them, and partly to save the am-

munition for shorter range, which he knew was sure to
come   Gen Lee, thinking he had silenced the Union
guns, immediately advanced a heavy line of infantry,
about 18,000 men, in command of Gen Pickett—hence
Pickett's charge   This column had to advance about
one mile to reach the Union position on Cemetery
Ridge, and every step was taken with the Union guns
pouring shot and shell into their faces, ploughing bloody
swaths through their already depleted columns   The
gaps would be immediately closed up, and on they
would come, with the steady step of veterans.   During
all this terrible ordeal there was not a shot fired from
their cannon, or from their advancing column.   When
within a few feet of the Union guns our infantry, which
had been lying flat on the ground, arose and poured
volley after volley into their thinned ranks, which lit-
terally melted away   Of that magnificent column,
truly " the pride of the Confederacy," only a few broken
fragments returned   Nearly every officer, except Gen.
Pickett, was either killed or wounded.   This ended the
great battle, as it should.   That night Gen. Lee retreated
towards the Potomac, leaving his dead unburied and
his wounded perishing for want of attention.

Gen. Lee marched to this field with 70,000 men of all
arms, while the force of Gen Meade was 82,000.   After
the first day's battle, in which the Union army lost over
5,000 prisoners, the armies were about equal in numbers.

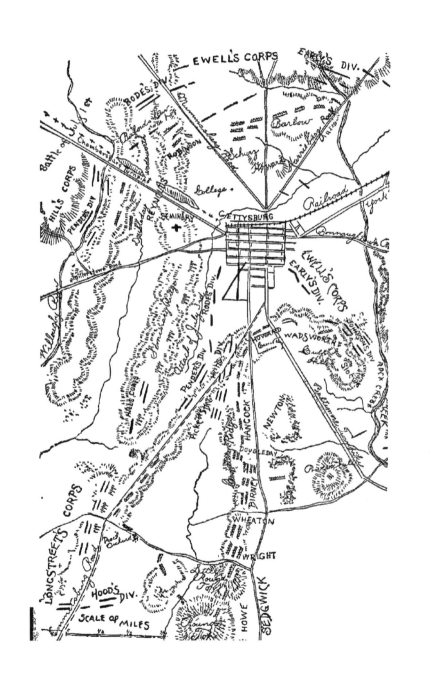

Comparative Losses by Corps and Brigades.

UNION CORPS.		CONFEDERATE CORPS	
First—8 brigades	6,052	First—13 brigades	7,354
Second—11 brigades .	4,351	Second—14 brigades	6,912
Third—7 brigades .	4,198	Third—15 brigades . .	6,649
Fifth—9 brigades.	2,186	Cavalry and reserve	10,706
Sixth—10 brigades	242		
Eleventh—7 brigades	3,801	Total . . .	31,621
Twelfth—7 brigades	1,082		
Artillery reserve . . .	425		
Cavalry, etc .	849		
Total	23,186		

The above figures include killed, wounded or missing. The killed and wounded in both armies amounted to 54,807

The brigades that suffered the most were—

Armstead's, C. S. A.	1,191	Iron brigade, U S A . .	1,153
Pittigrew's, C. S. A.	1,105	Robinson's Brigade, U. S. A	1,041
		Artillery, Wadsworth's	1,002

The following regiments sustained the heaviest losses.

26th N. C , Confederate	. 702	149th Pa , Union. .	336
24th Mich , Union . .	. 397	157th N Y , Union .	307
151st Pa , Union.	337		

The highest per cent of losses.

	Per cent.		Per cent.
26th N C., Confederate	. 88 5	24th Mich , Union . .	. 80
1st Minn, Union .	86	Each regiment mentioned above—over . .	70

Though larger forces had contended in battle, Gettysburg has few parallels in history. At Leipsic—"The Battle of the Nations"—The numbers were greater, the Allies having 330,000 and Bonaparte 175,000. Borodino was the bloodiest battle since the introduction of gunpowder in war ; there the killed and wounded were numerically greater than at Gettysburg, or at Waterloo, yet the per cent of loss was much less. The two great

R—7

battles of this century were Waterloo and Gettysburg,
and a striking comparison is shown between them.

At Gettysburg the Unionists had 82,000 men and 300
guns ; the Confederates, 70,000 men and 250 guns. The
Union loss was 23,186 men , the Confederate, 31,621
men

At Waterloo the French had 80,000 men and 252
guns , the Allies, 72,000 men and 186 guns. Bonaparte's
loss was 26,300 men , Wellington's, 23,185 men.

Gen. Meade's loss at Gettysburg was three times as
great as Gen Washington's loss during the entire Revolutionary War of seven years.

The combined Union and Confederate loss at Gettysburg was about double the combined American and
British loss during the Revolutionary War.

While the battle was in progress the cavalry on each
side took a prominent part on the flanks and rear. Stuart's Cavalry was continually annoying Gen Meade's
wagon trains and threatening his communication. The
Third Separate Brigade of the Eighth Corps was ordered
to guard the bridges and keep open communication with
Baltimore and Washington   The brigade was in command of Col. Samuel Graham, 3d Delaware Regiment,
and composed of the following troops 3d Delaware,
3d Maryland P. H. B , 1st Eastern Shore (Md.) Purnell
Legion, Battery L, 5th U. S. Artillery, and Loudoun
Rangers, and was stationed principally along the railroad   Part of the Loudoun Rangers was stationed at
the Relay House and part at Ellicott Mills.   The
latter place contains more pretty women than any place
of the same size in America. Perhaps it would be
unfair to the bashful corporals to give the names of
those that were more fortunate in the attention of the
ladies.   However, nearly every member of the company had a fair damsel at Ellicott Mills.   The company's mail was heavy to and from Ellicott afterwards.

"HEADQUARTERS OF THE ARMY,

"*Washington D. C., July* , 1863

"Capt. S. C. MEANS,

"*Comdg. Co. Va. Rangers,*

Relay House, B. & O. R. R :

"CAPTAIN You will, as soon as you have a sufficient number of your men remounted, proceed to the region threatened by the rebel forces, and take possession of and drive off into the nearest depot all horses suitable for cavalry, artillery, or baggage trains which are in any danger of falling into the hands of the enemy. Give receipts to the owners of these horses

"The receipts should contain a description of the horses, stating age, size, and whether fit for cavalry, artillery, or trains. These seizures should not be made in the immediate vicinity of the railroads unless there is imminent danger of the stock being taken by the enemy. The irritation inseparable from such operations would cause, perhaps, attempts to obstruct the track.

"Captain [Henry B.] Lacey, assistant quartermaster, who will hand you a copy of this order, will be accountable for the property thus taken, and will sign the receipts, which should also, when practicable, be countersigned by yourself He will accompany you.

"H. W HALLECK,

"*General-in-Chief*"

In compliance with these orders the command marched to Washington and camped at Tenallytown.

We marched up the Potomac, through Montgomery County, in carrying out the above orders.

If a farmer had but one horse it was not taken. These horses were taken without regard to ownership. Vouchers were given on the Quartermaster's Department, where the money could be obtained on presentation

The question of loyalty to the United States did not enter into the case Maryland, although somewhat divided on war issues, did not secede. Therefore, her

citizens were presumed to be loyal to the National
Government. Some citizens at first refused to part with
their stock, but, when shown an order from the Com-
mander-in Chief of the Army, made no further objec-
tions.

By the 15th of July the Rangers established camp at
Dripping Springs, near Point of Rocks This was a
most delightful camp, and proved to be the most enjoy-
able during our entire service. Located in a dense
forest on the eastern slope of the Catoctin Mountain, it
was laid out by clearing away the underbrush, making
a street about 75 feet wide by 200 feet long, with rows
of tents on each side of the street, and the officers' tents
at the western end, or up against the mountain, making
a beautiful court or grand boulevard. The court was
studded with shade trees This court was largely used
for morning roll call and general reception room for the
company's numerous lady visitors.

With such a pleasant place for a camp, it would seem
the Rangers ought to be at peace with all mankind, but
they were not. Our first parents were not contented
in the Garden of Eden, neither were the Rangers contented in this Garden of Eden of a camp " Chef de
cuisine " Moreland announced dinner. Coffee was made
in large camp kettles, and set out for every one to help
himself ; meat was cooked in large pans and set out in
the same way. Bread was also served in a similar
manner. The boys would get a tin cup full of coffee,
take bread and meat, and sit down and eat. On one
occasion William Bull accidently upset Corporal Sam.
Tritapoe's coffee, the corporal in turn upset Bull's coffee.
As it was an easy matter to get a fight out of either, they
locked horns The entire company yelled " free fight,"
" hands off," etc. Jock Cooper said he would shoot
the first man that would part them. They broke
down several splendid shade trees Sergt. Bull got a

black eye, while Corporal Tritapoe got his new "biled" shirt rather recklessly ventilated , in the mean time all the coffee was drank, leaving the pugilists to finish on water.   The honor of both was amply vindicated. The Rangers were fighting for principle, and as there was more or less principle involved in a cup of coffee, there was no reason why they should not fight for that as well as to fight Mosby's men, who were entirely devoid of principle   A few days later Henry C. Hough ("by daggy") and Robert S. Harper brought this beautiful camp in reproach again by pounding each other in the face "about oats."   The blood flowed freely—the battle was fierce but brief.   Perhaps it was a small matter to fight about, but was a big question with the horse that got the oats.

We had one recruit at this beautiful camp, Thomas Fouch.

Capt. Means issued an order here, his authority for which was doubtful.   It was a kind of general conscript law for Loudoun County.   A portion of the company was sent into Loudoun and notified quite a number of citizens of proper age that the time was ripe for them to enlist in defence of the Union.   They were given the choice as to the command they would enlist in, although the captain expected the great mass would join the Rangers, and undoubtedly they would had the matter come to a choice.   The order was short-lived however, as there was but the one lot summoned, although several of Loudoun's loyal sons came to our camp to confer with Capt. Means about it, namely, Samuel Compher, Thomas J Loy, Samuel Wenner and others

July 20th the command went to Waterford, accompanying Gen. Meade's advance.   The Rangers remained here for several days.   Our command was a great favorite with the intensely loyal citizens of the Quaker village   The officers of the 24th Michigan

gave a grand ball at Waterford, and some faint idea of
what the Northern Union soldiers thought of this village may be learned by the following, which is taken
from the History of the 24th Michigan, a regiment that
lost more men at Gettysburg than any other regiment
that participated in that great battle.

"Waterford, a most beautifully embowered and intensely loyal village. It seemed strange to find so patriotic a place in the Confederate dominions. That
evening merry maidens of the place with elastic step
tripped the fantastic toe with our army officers. The
streets were lined with smiles and beauty. Windows
and balconies were filled with matrons, maidens, and
children, who waved handkerchiefs and the starry flag,
and cheered on the Union troops with many a hurrah
for the Union. God bless Waterford!"

ARMY CROSSING THE POTOMAC ON PONTOON BRIDGES AT BRUNSWICK.

The Rangers returned to camp at Point of Rocks the
last of July.

As has been previously stated, the Rangers were not
so fortunate as to have a hospital or even a doctor, and
as a result, when any of the boys needed pills, or quinine

they had to be sent away to be dosed. About August 1, Sergt. Joseph T. Divine and Daniel Harper were on the sick-list, and were sent to the hospital at Frederick, and placed in the same ward with Lieut Charles Beatty, of Cole's Cavalry, and Isaac Walker, of Company I, 1st Maryland P. H B. A few doses sent the boys to Convalescent Hospital at Patterson Park, Baltimore When the boys had sufficiently recovered to be sent to Camp Distribution, near Alexandria, they were taken out late one evening and marched from the park to the Union Relief Building, near Camden Station, in Baltimore, where they were given an excellent supper. This will be pleasantly remembered by many old soldiers of the Army of the Potomac as the place where they were supplied with a square meal free.

There seemed to be no provision made for sending the boys away until the next day. What to do with them that night was not a very great question for the nation, yet it was an immense question for the boys. The provost marshal solved it by locking them up in jail until morning. Sergt. Joseph Divine says when the jailer turned his ponderous key the clanking of the lock sent a chill down his spinal column that will be remembered to the end of his days The next day they were put on cars and sent to Camp Stoneman, near Washington, and from there forwarded to their commands.

The 1st of August a squad of the Rangers crossed the Potomac on foot, going to Taylortown and Downey's Mill, crossed the Catoctin Mountain, going back by the Furnace In the rounds we captured two rebels, one of them Charles Dawson, of the 8th Virginia. Dawson had just come from Gettysburg, and had as much of the Confederacy as he could digest. He did not want to be sent to prison, because in due time he would be exchanged and sent to his regiment again, but wanted to remain in Maryland without taking the oath of alle-

giance   His sisters came and visited him at our camp.
He was finally sent to Fort McHenry

September 11 the Rangers, accompanied by Cole's
Cavalry, were ordered to Loudoun on an extended raid.
The night of the 12th we camped at Waterford   While
here Capt. Means learned from a friend where Company
B of White's Confederate Cavalry would be the next
day

We left Waterford about daylight, Sunday, the 13th,
marching direct to the top of the Catoctin Mountain,
where the command was divided, Lieut. Atwell, of Company B, with about twenty men, taking a path down
the mountain, entering the Gray farm from the north,
while Capts. Means and Cole, with Sergt. Edward White
in command of the advance guard, single-filed down the
mountain and came out a little southwest of the Gray
residence.   About 125 men, mostly of Company B, of
White's Confederate Cavalry, were in the woods 100
yards west of the Gray mansion, asleep, having arrived
just before daylight.   It was their intention to rest all
day and at night cross the Potomac into Maryland and
take forcible possession of two new stores that had
been recently opened.   By this method the goods could
be obtained on "long time"—but the Rangers played
havoc with their plans.   The squad with Lieut. Atwell
arrived about 9 o'clock a. m.   Entering through the
barnyard, where two rebels were sitting, Gatton and
Broyles of Point of Rocks, Atwell picked them up,
while Sergt. Jim Beatty, Henry Hough, Sam Tritapoe,
John Densmore, Sergt. Flem Anderson and others
rushed immediately to the spot where "our friends,
the enemy," were quietly napping   The boys went
in, yelling and shooting, completely taking them by
surprise, scattering them barefooted, bareheaded, and
some of them barebacked, in every direction   Many
of them left their horses tied to trees, darted through

Sergt. JOHN W. FORSYTHE, Co. B.

JAMES W. HARRISON, Co. B.

the bushes and escaped. Capt. Means' crowd, approaching from the southwest, were about two minutes late, otherwise we would have bagged the whole lot. Lieut. Crown, who was in command of the rebels, was at the Gray residence and endeavored to escape through the garden, but was wounded in the leg and was captured. We captured both of their officers—Lieuts Crown and Dorsey—and 16 privates, wounding one severely—Tom Tilton—and three or four slightly Dorsey and Tilton were captured at the Swan residence Dorsey was a dyed-in-the-wool Maryland rebel and of a very haughty spirit When made prisoner he swelled up like a turkey gobbler and proclaimed, " I am a gentleman and an officer, and wish to be recognized and treated as such." He was slightly deformed, his left arm was a little the shortest, and the fingers on that hand were about one inch long, although he had perfect use of them This company was from Maryland, and claimed to be fighting for their homes. Their position was made ridiculous by the fact of their being fugitives from the laws of both State and Nation during the entire war. Corporals Robert W. Hough, J T McCutcheon, Charles Snoots, and others, gave chase to a squad of the fugitives, who took refuge in Fort Hill, that was erected in defense of Leesburg early in the war, by Gen. D. H. Hill Three of White's men were captured in the fort—one, a brother of Lieut Crown—who, in his haste to get away, was wearing but one boot. He had a slight deformity—a hair lip While each member of the Rangers present on this occasion did his whole duty, yet we think the following deserve special recognition for their conspicuous bravery and aggressiveness, viz. : Sergts. James Beatty, Edward T. White, and Flemon Anderson, Privates Henry Hough, John Densmore, Corp. Samuel Tritapoe, Charles Snoots, and Mike Ryan. In addition to the prisoners we also captured about thirty horses and equipments, with about the same number of small arms. We also captured several pairs of women's shoes, some dry goods, and a copy of Shakespeare, left by the fleet-footed Marylanders Several of our boys were hurt in charging through the thick woods Charles Snoot's horse fell, giving him a painful wound. While this fight was in progress, Col. Lige White, with four men, was at his farm, about two miles east, near White's Ferry This affair was humiliating to Col. White, because it was one of his best companies that was caught napping, without the slightest sign of a picket or camp-guard posted. After this affair was over our column moved on to near Ball's Bluff, where a band of rebels was routed, capturing two. We passed on through Lees-burg and west over the mountains, through Waterford, to Harper's Ferry and down the towpath to camp at Dripping Springs.

Sergt M. S Gregg, Joseph T. Ritchie, and others, who were captured at the Point of Rocks June 17, were exchanged and returned to the company.

The pickets on the Potomac had rigid orders not to allow any one to approach from the Virginia side without dismounting before reaching the shore One evening Capt Means went over to the Island, remaining until after dark. On coming back "old Sam" Fry was on picket. He challenged Capt. Means, demanding—"Dismount, advance and give the countersign." Means yelled out, "Oh, you know me, let me ride out" Old Sam roared out · "I know nobody while on picket ; dismount quickly ; advance and give the countersign." It was no use to parley with old Sam. Capt. Means dismounted and waded out like a little man

September 1, 1863, Lieut. Joseph E. Thrasher, 1st Maryland P H. B., and about twelve of the Rangers, were ordered to near Lovettsville to look after a rebel

picket post. On our arrival we found the enemy had
vacated about twenty four hours before. We camped
for the night at Lovettsville. Here happened one of
the many unfortunate and deplorable incidents of the
war. Charles Spring was on picket. About 12 o'clock
midnight a horseman was approaching. The picket
challenged, but he kept advancing, as there was but
one person approaching Spring did not shoot but called
Lieut Thrasher, who challenged the horseman three
times, but still he kept advancing Lieut Thrasher
fired with his revolver, when the rider fell from his
horse into the road. He proved to be Peter Hickman,
who did not understand the meaning of the challenge.
He was a Union man and a most exemplary citizen.
The affair was greatly regretted by the Rangers and
their friends

CHAPTER VIII.

BACK TO HARPER'S FERRY—RECRUITING COMPANY B—THE AF-
FAIR AT NEERSVILLE—CAMP MOVED TO CHARLESTOWN—
SCOUTING IN THE VALLEY—THE CHARLESTOWN FIGHT—
RECRUITING COMPANIES C AND D

September 20 the command moved to Harpers Ferry,
camping on Magazine Heights, Camp Hill The 30th,
Lieut Gover, with 30 men of Company A and six men
of Company B, went over "Between the Hills," (Blue
Ridge and Catoctin Mountains). At Neersville the numerous horse tracks in the road showed evidence of a
body of cavalry in that section. As ours were the only
Federal troops near, the inference was that the enemy
was near. After scouting around for about two hours
our column started back towards Harpers Ferry. F P
Rinker and James Stoneburner hitched their horses to
a fence and went into an orchard to get apples. Sergts.
Robert Graham, James W. Gregg, John P Hickman,

privates Charles H. Snoots, John S. Densmore, Joseph T. Ritchie, and the writer started in the direction of the Blue Ridge, where the horse tracks seemed to lead.   We came to a place where a negro man was making cider—a genuine rebel negro.   He knew all about the rebels, but would not tell, even when Sergt. Graham threatened to kill him if he did not reveal their whereabouts, but he was immovable.   The boys drank freely of cider, and Hickman and the writer filled their canteens   On going back to the column we had left on the road going towards Harpers Ferry we ran across a small squad of rebels. James W Gregg and Charles H. Snoots were some distance in the advance, and opened fire.   The rebels retired slowly into John Grubb's barnyard, where Gregg and Snoots rushed in after them.   The rebels now halted, but kept shooting at Gregg and Snoots, who were also shooting at very close range.   Suddenly a column of rebel cavalry came out of the woods east of the barn in perfect line and opened fire on Gregg and Snoots   The balance of Graham's squad, who had not advanced far enough to be drawn into the trap, turned and endeavored to rejoin Gover, whom they had left a few minutes before on the Harpers Ferry pike.   Gregg and Snoots had a hand-to-hand fight, and, strange as it may seem, both got away and rode into Harpers Ferry   Gregg was badly wounded in the right thigh and in the right hand, and his horse, "Old Sam" was shot through the neck. Charles Snoots was wounded in the neck and his horse shot in the breast.

The rebel column now filed to the right and came out on the Harpers Ferry pike and struck Gover's column in the rear and threw them into some confusion.   The latter retired towards the Ferry.   In this affair Company A had three or four wounded , we lost two prisoners, Rinker and Stoneburner, who were getting apples.   Company B lost one prisoner, Sergt Reuben Stypes.   James

W. Gregg's wounds were quite serious, he was taken to the General Hospital at Harpers Ferry, where they were dressed and cared for for several weeks.

The rebels had three wounded, Lieut. Cunningham being wounded in the breast by J W. Gregg.

This rebel force was commanded by Capt. F. Dowdell, of White's Cavalry, with Company C and part of Company A, with one company, 1st Virginia Cavalry, commanded by Lieut. Cunningham of that regiment.

Michael Mullen was commissioned October 3 to recruit Company C, with offices established at Harpers Ferry. October 12, George Swope joined Company A. October 11, Lieut Gover, with 30 men, was ordered to Charlestown on special duty. Col. Benjamin L Simpson of the 9th Maryland (nine-month's troops), was in command. The garrison consisted of 9th Maryland, 375 men; about 20 men of Company I, 6th Michigan Cavalry, in command of Lieut. Moon, and 30 men of the Loudoun Rangers. Capt. Summers, of Cole's Cavalry, while raiding near Summit Point October 8, was attacked by a part of the 23d Virginia Cavalry, in command of Maj Robert. White, who was concealed behind a stone fence. When Capt Summers approached within short range the enemy rose up and fired into the company, killing Capt Summers and several of his men. The attack was so cowardly and sudden that it threw the men into confusion, compelling them to let their wounded fall into the hands of the enemy This company was left without officers, and the Rangers above referred to were ordered to relieve them, and were put to active scouting in the direction of Winchester and Front Royal. Gen. Imboden's brigade lay at the latter place, 40 miles southwest of Charlestown Capt. Lefferts, of the 1st New York (Lincoln) Cavalry, with one company, left Martinsburg 16th and marched to Berryville, where they ran into Imboden's brigade, who captured three of the New Yorkers—Jerome Bell, Dick Moran, and Frenchy. These three were afterwards tentmates of some of the Rangers on Belle Isle.

After this brush with Imboden, Capt. Lefferts went to Charlestown and reported this Confederate force to Col. Simpson, who refused to fall back to Harpers Ferry The colonel did not believe this force would attack Charlestown ; and, if they did, he felt sure he could hold his own against cavalry, as he was not aware the enemy had infantry and artillery. At early dawn, Sunday, October 18th, Sergt. Beatty's picket (M. H Best) was driven in About ten or twelve shots were fired, and one minute later that harsh and discordant, yet old familiar rebel yell was heard east and north of town, particularly on the Harpers Ferry pike To the old soldier no explanation was necessary ; he too well understood the significance of this early morning call. The town was surrounded by Gen. Imboden's brigade, of the following troops .

18th Virginia Cavalry, about 500 men ,
62d Virginia Mounted Infantry, about 475 men ,
41st Virginia Cavalry, Robert White, about 200 men ;
Harry Gilmore, about 325 men ,
12th Virginia Cavalry, about 250 men ;
McClanahan's Battery, 150 men.   Total, 1,900.

The Rangers mounted and reported to Col. Simpson, at the court-house, for orders. The colonel informed Lieut Gover the infantry was fortified and would remain in the court-house, and, as a matter of necessity, the cavalry would be compelled to take care of themselves. These somewhat vague orders left the future action of the Rangers entirely discretionary with Lieut. Gover. The 9th Maryland had cut portholes through the walls of the court-house and jail and were prepared to receive their morning callers.

In the meantime Gen. Imboden had sent in a flag of

truce, demanding an immediate surrender of the town.
Col. Simpson sent word back if he (Gen. Imboden)
wanted the place to come in and take it. The Maryland boys were comfortably housed in their citadel and
did not borrow trouble over the situation ; but the cavalry were not quite so comfortably situated.

Lieut. Gover formed his 30 men in fours and ordered
a charge down the Harpers Ferry pike, endeavoring to
cut their way out. In a strip of woods, on the out-
edge of town, we encountered the 18th Virginia Cavalry and part of the 62d Virginia Mounted Infantry,
who poured volley after volley into our column. Most
of the horses in the front fours were shot, which somewhat blocked the pike and caused the column to slightly
oblique to the left. This was slightly to our advantage,
as the enemy seemed fewer to the left On we went,
emptying our revolvers at the enemy. We finally succeeded in breaking through their lines, but not without
considerable loss. Out of our thirty men we lost 17
wounded and prisoners, as follows :

A J. Cox,	A. C Hawk,
J. H. Beatty,	George Nogle,
J. T. McCutcheon,	S. Shackelford,
Joseph Magaha,	Richard Virts,
James Daily,	H Stewart,
H. W. Hoover,	George Swope,
Joseph Waters,	P. A. Davis,
W. H. Angelow,	Briscoe Goodhart
Thomas Dixon,	

Nearly every horse in the command was shot going
out. Sergt. James H Beatty was shot twice, and his
horse three times

Daniel Harper was very badly wounded in the thigh
and left on the field by the enemy

Sergt Flemon B Anderson was wounded in the hand,
but went through to Harpers Ferry.

George Davis had his shoulder painfully hurt by falling against a tree when his horse was shot. He also got a bullet through his boot, his horse got up and carried him to the Ferry and died.

Joseph T. Ritchie's horse was shot, but carried Joe about four miles and died

George W. Nogle was dangerously hurt in the shoulder, neck and face, his horse was shot, and both horse and rider were run over by the two sets of fours following.

John McDavitt got a bullet through his hat, but he went through.

John P. Hickman's horse was shot dead at the first volley, and fell at the edge of the woods. J. P. H. went back to the 9th Maryland and got a horse and went out with Col Simpson and others.

"Report of Capt. Samuel C Means, Virginia (Union) Rangers

"HARPERS FERRY, W. VA.
"October 20, 1863

"SIR I respectfully report the loss in the fight at Charlestown, on Sunday, October 18, as 17 men prisoners and 1 wounded ; also 19 full sets of arms and horse equipments, 1 wagon, 4 sets of harness, and 23 horses killed and taken, besides several badly shot, now in camp

"Very respectfully, your obedient servant,
"SAML. C. MEANS,
"Captain, Comdg. Independent Virginia Rangers.
"To General SULLIVAN."

While the Rangers were taking care of themselves, as intimated by Col. Simpson, Gen. Imboden had sent in the second flag of truce, demanding a surrender, and had planted four pieces of artillery 200 yards north of the court-house, and immediately began throwing shells into that building This sealed the fate of Col. Simp-

Corp. D. J. HARPER, Co. A.

son. The Maryland boys were now compelled to leave
their stronghold and go into the streets. The rebels
had the other two pieces of McClanahan's battery
planted on Main Street west of the court-house to open
on the Marylanders when they left the court-house, but
the streets were now filled with citizens, which somewhat changed the programme.

Col. Simpson marched his men down the Harpers
Ferry pike and formed in line of battle in the field
where John Brown was hung (December 2, 1859), their
line facing the woods where the Rangers had met with
such a warm reception a few minutes before. The
enemy had massed the most of its forces in these woods
and opened a heavy fire on the Marylanders, who were
marching in that direction. The battle was of short
duration   After two or three rounds the 9th Maryland
surrendered with 365 men   The regiment has been
somewhat criticised for surrendering thus early in the
fight, yet no one knew better than Col Simpson that
he did not have a ghost of a chance of success without
artillery and over five to one against him

After the regiment had surrendered, . Color Sergt.
Benjamin Swearer took the National colors from the
flagstaff and wrapped it around his body, under his
clothing, and carried it to Richmond unnoticed by the
rebels. While the prisoners were disrobed and being
searched in Pemberton prison, by a clever trick the
sergeant eluded the searchers and carried the National
banner to Belle Isle, where he secretly but quietly
guarded his precious treasure during that memorable
winter. On being paroled in March he carried it away
from Richmond. After being transported from the
rebel steamboat "Wm. Allison" to the Union steamer
"City of New York," and not until the latter had departed for Annapolis, Md., did Sergt. Swearer make his
secret known, displaying the emblem of liberty to his

R—8

fellow prisoners, with cheer after cheer for the star spangled banner.

This was the first time the regiment was ever under fire. Having been mustered in at Baltimore August 17, just sixty days previous. Col. Simpson's action about the time the regiment surrendered is open to criticism Col Simpson, Lt. Col Clawdsley, Maj. Church, Surg Morgan, Ast. Surg Kemp, Chaplain Gray, of the 9th Maryland, and John P. Hickman of the Rangers, by a dash to the left, crossing the pike and through fields in the direction of Duffields, succeeded in getting through the line unnoticed, and arrived at the Ferry in safety.

The cannonading was distinctly heard at Harpers Ferry, eight miles east, where the troops were preparing for dress parade. The 17th Indiana Battery of six guns, in command of Capt. Minor, Cole's Cavalry, one company of the 6th Michigan Cavalry, and what was left of the Loudoun Rangers, making in all about 300 men, immediately started for the scene of action. Fifty minutes from the time they left the Ferry they had opened fire on the rebels south of Charlestown The Confederates would make a stand until our troops would advance to close quarters when they would fall back and take a new position. This fire-and-fall-back fighting was continued all day Our cavalry and artilery fought like Trojans, but did not have sufficient numbers to recapture the prisoners.

The 17th Indiana Battery did most excellent service on this occasion. They went into action eight times during the day, firing 810 shell and case shot, and 30 rounds of cannister. They also came near losing two guns, being saved by the dash and stubborn fighting of Cole's Cavalry. Our force was in command of Col. Wells, of the 34th Massachusetts Infantry, who hurried on with the cavalry and artillery His regiment did not arrive until about 5 o'clock p. m. near Berryville, having marched 18 miles. Our force was now about 700. The Confederates made a final stand just before sundown. The 34th Massachusetts went into action and did most excellent service, completely routing the enemy, who were saved by the approach of darkness. The 34th Massachusetts lost about 12 killed and quite a number wounded in this final charge of the day.

The 10th Maryland Infantry, encamped on Maryland Heights, started early for the scene of action, but having four miles further to march did not get further than Charlestown, remaining there until the next day, October 19. This regiment saved Charlestown from destruction by fire during the night of October 18.

Col. Wells' command returned to Harpers Ferry that night, arriving about 12 o'clock (midnight), with 21 prisoners. In addition to this, the enemy left about 40 dead and badly wounded on the field. Our loss during the day, after the arrival of the troops from Harpers Ferry, was 22 killed and about 50 wounded.

We captured during the retreat of the enemy five wagons and one battery forge.

Cole's Cavalry lost one of their best officers, Capt. Houk, Company H, killed, and several of that company wounded. Company K lost four killed, and several wounded

Col. Simpson felt that he had been unjustly criticised about the affair and requested a court of inquiry to determine his responsibility in the premises.

In compliance with this request, Gen B. F. Kelley, Commander of the Department, convened the court November 13, at Harpers Ferry, which was composed of the following persons :

Col. W. P. Maulsby, 1st Maryland P. H. B.,

Maj. Frank A. Rolf, 1st Massachusetts Heavy Artillery;

Maj. W. B. Curtis, 12th West Virginia Infantry.

The court examined the case at considerable length, and reported that Col. Simpson should not be held responsible for the disaster that befel the regiment and the other commands present on that occasion, and the papers were forwarded to the Department Commander for his approval

Gen. Kelley reviewed the case, but could not approve of the findings of the court, and forwarded the same to Secretary of War, Edwin M. Stanton, with the recommendation that Col. Simpson be dismissed from the service of the United States

The Hon Secretary of War referred the entire affair to Judge Advocate General Holt, who reviewed it from a legal-military standpoint. Gen. Holt concurred in the recommendation of the court of inquiry, and, upon this report, the Secretary of War ordered Col. Simpson to be assigned to duty, which ended the case.

Col Simpson and those officers who escaped with him from Charlestown were mustered out February 23, 1864.

It is but fair to state that Col Simpson was one of the few early Baltimore loyalists who were unmovable in their loyalty to the flag of the country. He rendered valuable service to Gen. Butler early in 1861, when the latter took possession of Baltimore.

October 19th, George H. Waters joined the company His brother Joe was captured the day before at Charlestown.

October 26th, Lieut. Keyes with 20 men was ordered on a scout to Leesburg to intercept and capture a squad of rebels who were engaged in collecting supplies for the Confederacy. Approaching Big Spring the enemy was routed ; Samuel E. Tritapoe and M. H. Best, the two Invincibles, were in the advance and captured two Johnnies, Gen. Rust and Capt Suttle These two officers belonged to the Confederate Quartermaster Department. Gen. Rust was a graduate of West Point and a classmate of Gen. Sherman As this squad approached Leesburg, the enemy was encountered again, and one prisoner was captured, John Rinker, who was believed to belong to the Loudoun Cavalry. On this raid Samuel E. Tritapoe's horse fell while jumping a ditch, painfully injuring Tritapoe's hip.

The Genesis of Company B

The first effort put forth to recruit a battalion took tangible shape in the spring of 1863, while Company A was camped at Brunswick. Capt. Patterson, of Maryland, a former drillmaster of Company A (related to the Emperor Napoleon I. of France by marriage), was commissioned captain ; Mr Lovett, of Jefferson County, W Va., was 1st lieutenant ; William Bull was to be first sergeant. Recruiting offices were opened at Martinsburg, W. Va. There was issued to the company arms and uniforms for 50 men. Capt. Patterson was offered a better position in the Quartermaster Department. Lieut. Lovett became involved in some stock contracts, and the recruits, about 12 men, disbanded The only one re-enlisted in Company A was William Bull He came to Company A wearing first sergeant stripes Although a private in Company A he was generally known as Sergt. Bull, or Patterson's Bull.

After the Gettysburg campaign, while Company A was camped at Dripping Springs, near Point of Rocks, Md., the effort to recruit a battalion was renewed. Late in July Michael Mullen and Charles M Atwell, both of Company A, began to recruit Company B, and opened recruiting offices at Harpers Ferry and at Sandy Hook, and recruited about 20 men ; August 20 Charles F. Anderson, of Company A, began to recruit Company C, and established headquarters at Lovettsville, Va., where he recruited George H Hickman, Thomas Dewire, Phil Prichard, Hiram Casaught (Irish John), S. W. Goodhart, Peter W Fry, George W. Loy and Samuel White.

About the same time Sergt. James W Virts and Corporal James W. Grubb, both of Cole's Maryland Cavalry, began to recruit Company D, and opened recruiting offices at Frederick, Md., where they secured about 30 recruits. In September Companies B, C and D were ordered to Harpers Ferry

Sergt. Virts was taken sick and remained so for about one month, and on his recovery Capt. Vernon ordered him back to his old command, Company A, 1st Maryland P. H. B. Cavalry

November 1, while camped on Magazine Heights, Camp Hill, Bolivar, Capt. Anderson slipped and fell over the heights, about 200 feet, and was killed

Some weeks after this Capt. Mullen was taken prisoner, and died on his return to Camp Parole, at Annapolis, Md., which left all the companies without commanders and in somewhat a confused state   James W. Grubb, in the meantime, had recruited quite an addition to Company D, and Atwell held Company B together, while Company C was left without a commissioned officer

Luther W. Slater, formerly of Company A, still suffering from the wounds he received at Waterford, who had shown himself a patriot on more than one occasion, again came to the rescue and commanded Company C until they recruited sufficient numbers to elect a captain.   He did this without any compensation whatever, simply to keep the company from disbanding

In November Capt. Means ordered Companies B, C, and D consolidated, and out of this trio grew Company B anew, electing the following officers : Captain, James W. Grubb , 1st Lieut., Charles M. Atwell , 2d Lieut., Augustus C. Rhodes ; First Sergeant, George H.

Hickman. As was anticipated, the new consolidation was a disappointment to some, and a few recruits from companies B and C withdrew and left the service.

The new company was officered with first-class material, all having had experience in the service. They numbered about 60 men, and presented a bold front to the enemy on all occasions.

November 1 George V. Kern joined Company A. Kern was of excellent material, and made a good soldier

Early in December the command moved to Brunswick, establishing depots for the reception and purchasing of hay from the citizens of Virginia for Uncle Sam

CHAPTER IX.

BACK AT POINT OF ROCKS—IN WINTER QUARTERS—"GATHERING HAY"—MOVED TO THE FURNACE—CAPT MEANS LEAVES THE SERVICE—ORDERED TO WEST VIRGINIA—THE SECOND FIGHT AT WATERFORD

Early in January the command moved to Point of Rocks, going into winter quarters. A depot for purchasing hay was also established here The presses for baling were located on the Virginia side of the Potomac. Every day that the weather and the condition of the roads would admit, teams, with an escort, were sent into Virginia to collect hay and corn for the Quartermaster's Department Citizens were given vouchers on Uncle Sam for their supplies This "hay soldiering" proved exceptionably pleasant for the boys; while they were very diligent in collecting forage for the Government, they were equally diligent collecting information as to when citizens of Loudoun would give dances and various other entertainments

The Rangers had a weakness for such amusements Nearly all the young men were in the war, but the supply of young ladies, both as to quantity and quality,

seemed almost inexhaustible. Under these circumstances, and with some slight effort, the Rangers were
sure·of lady friends   Perhaps it would be wearisome to
relate the numerous episodes of these parties during the
winter.   One is too good to be lost, and it may serve as a
pointer for the actors in the next war.

A ball was to be given at one of the many pleasant
farm houses of Loudoun.   Six of the Rangers were
invited to be present, namely, James W. Gregg, John
P. Hickman, F. B. Anderson, Daniel J. Harper, George
Hickman, and Henry C. Hough ("by daggy ").   It
was understood, of course, that certain young ladies,
especial friends to the above, would be present to trip
the fantastic toe with their "friends."   During the
night a deep snow fell, making traveling impossible
without some kind of a conveyance.   It was war times.
Horses and sleighs were as scarce as white blackbirds.
How the ladies were to get home the next day was
perplexing to the fair sex.   Finally the Rangers happily
solved the question.   They proposed to take the ladies
home on horseback   The suggestion was popular
Each fellow adjusted his saddle blanket to meet the
necessities of the occasion, and taking up his "best
friend" behind him started for their homes.   The
ladies were not provided with riding costumes, and, of
course, good etiquette suggested single file.   It was
rather a picturesque procession, but as the snow was
deep there would probably be no one out to witness
the caravan.   When about half way home with their
precious burdens Lieut. Keyes, with a portion of the
command, was encountered going on a raid   In passing,
the lieutenant very politely recognized each of the
dancers with a "Good morning," calling each by name.
This was taken up by the entire command, with a
"Good morning, Jim," "Good morning, J. P. H.," etc.
The dancers blushed almost beyond recognition   The

Sergt. JOHN P. HICKMAN, Co. A.

ladies hid their faces from view.   Daniel J Harper said
it seemed to him they were about three hours in passing
the company   The ladies were safely taken to their
homes, and the boys then followed the command, over-
taking them near Milltown.

While Capt. Means, with a portion of Companies A
and B, was raiding in Loudoun in February, he learned
of a detachment of Mosby's men being near Wheatland.
An advance guard, consisting of Flemon Anderson,
George Hickman, Dave Hough, Sergt Forsythe, Company B, and William Bull, was sent out.   It was learned
the enemy was at Washington Vandeventer's enjoying a
dance.   The advance was sent to the house while the
captain and squad remained near the barn   William
Bull and Flemon Anderson entered the front door, when
they received the fire from seven men concealed in the
hall   These two men opened fire on the rebels, driving them out in the garden, where one, by the name of
Braden, was killed, two wounded, and four made prisoners.   One of the ladies, a Miss Braden, was slightly
wounded.

The small-pox broke out in our camp late in February.   John P. Hickman, George P Davis, M. H.
Best, Ed. Snyder, Charles Stout and Wilson Shackelford
were attacked with the disease.   Stout and Shackelford died in the small-pox hospital near Weverton,
Md.   The others recovered and returned to duty in the
spring.

Wilson Shackelford was buried near the hospital.
After the war his body was removed to the National
Cemetery at Antietam, Md.

Charles Stout was buried in the family burying
ground of John Brown, near the Valley Church.

During the month of January Capt. Means went to
Washington.   While at the War Office he heard Secretary Stanton inquiring about a fresh cow.   The cap-

tain modestly suggested that Loudoun County produced some of the finest stock in the State, and if the Secretary would allow him he would send him a fine milch cow. The suggestion met with Mr. Stanton's approval. On Capt Means' return to camp he sent a small squad to Loudoun, with instructions to have one of the best cows to be found purchased and delivered to him at the Point The animal was delivered according to directions and loaded on the express car to be sent to Washington. William Bull, of Company A, who had formerly lived in Washington and was well acquainted with the streets, was ordered to go on the same train and deliver the animal at the residence of Secretary Stanton.

Capt. Means stepped into the telegraph office and wired the Secretary, as follows :

" I send you to day Sergt. Bull with cow and calf
      " Very respectfully,
               " Capt. S. C. MEANS."

By an annoying blunder in transmitting the telegram the word "sergt." was omitted, making the telegram read
      "I send you to-day bull with cow and calf.
         " Very respectfully,
               " Capt S C. MEANS."

In due time Sergt. Bull presented himself at the War Office, and on making himself known, the Secretary broke into a furious rage and asked, "What kind of a captain have you ? What do I want with a bull ? Take them all back ; I will receive none of them." This brusque reception somewhat weakened the sergeant's knees, but he attempted an explanation. The Secretary broke out more savagely then ever " Don't want any explanation. Take them all back."

The sergeant retired to the corridor, where he met a

lieutenant on duty there and explained matters to that officer. The lieutenant went in and assured the Secretary there was no bull in the case, that the sergeant's name was Bull, and that a fine cow and calf were delivered at the Secretary's residence. Mr. Stanton was glad to learn the true state of affairs, and called Mr. Bull in and presented him with ten dollars, and asked him to present his acknowledgments to Capt. Means

Early in February the camp was moved to the Catoctin Furnace, where the following recruits joined Company A· John Coats (Coats-a-mish), Charles Virts, Charles E Curry, Charles F. Moreland, Jonathan Myers, William H. Hardy

In the spring of 1864, Gen Franz Sigel was assigned to the command of the Department of West Virginia, with headquarters at Cumberland, Md The Department embraced all the troops west of the Monocacy River in Maryland and east of the Ohio River.

The last of March Capt. Means was ordered with his command to Parkersburg, W. Va., to be consolidated with the 3d West Virginia Cavalry, when the regiment was to move to Charleston, W. Va, and be assigned to duty under Gen. Crook.

Capt. Means refused to comply with this order, because it was in direct violation of the instructions of the Hon. Edwin M. Stanton, Secretary of War, which was that the Rangers were recruited for special service, and to be subject to his orders only.

This order led to quite a spirited correspondence covering dates from April 1 to 26, and participated in by Gens. Crook, Averill, Sigel and Weber, and Capts. Means and Bamford, and as a result Capt. Means left the service April 13, 1864.

Whether Capt. Means was right or wrong, it is gratifying to know he was sustained by the Secretary of War (See final dispatches to Capt Bamford and Gen. Crook.)

" Headquarters,
" *Harpers Ferry, April 25, 1864.*
" Captain Bamford,
    " *Provost-Marshal, Point of Rocks :*

" Lieut. Keyes, commanding Independent Virginia Rangers, will remain as at present until further orders, the order for their movement having been countermanded

" By order of Brig Gen. Max Weber :
        " Saml. F. Woods,
          " *Assistant Adjutant-General* "

" Cumberland, *April 26, 1864.*
" Brigadier-General Crook,
    " *Charleston ·*

" The orders directing Capt. Means' companies to proceed to Charleston have been revoked under instructions from the Secretary of War, they having been recruited for conditional service. The companies formerly at Buckhannon left some days ago to report to you.

" By order :
        " T. Melvin,
        " *Assistant Adjutant-General.*"

Lieut. Keyes was promoted to captain ; 2d Lieut. Gover to 1st lieutenant ; First Sergeant Flemon Anderson was in the line of promotion to 2d lieutenant, but Capt. Keyes wanted Sergt Robert Graham for that position. The Lovettsville and Taylortown boys wanted Anderson. An election was held, and Sergt. Graham was declared elected 2d lieutenant by a slight majority. The Anderson men reluctantly accepted this edict, yet not without some slight murmuring, as it seems the four men in the hospital were enthusiastic Anderson men, and would have more than elected him, but Capt. Keyes declined to allow their votes to be counted However, Graham proved to be a popular officer, and rendered good service.

The Great Unknown — "The Government Mule."

A most excellent authority has declared had there been no mule there would have been no war. This statement, though somewhat reckless, contains much truth. The fact is the army mule in war is as effective as the army musket—both have good "kicking qualities," and when actively engaged have been known to create desolation and woe Of the two, perhaps the mule is most to be dreaded ; he is always loaded and ready for action, and will let fly without the slightest pretext or excuse.

While gathering hay the company picked up a large mule, bearing Uncle Sam's familiar trade-mark, "U. S " To the boys this was "*prima facie*" evidence of ownership , so we brought him along. When near the Catoctin Furnace the column halted to feed and get something to eat   While the horses were eating Sergt Ed White, a good judge of horseflesh, and somewhat of a horse jockey, and a good rider, saddled up the mule and mounted him, with a view of testing his adaptability to cavalry service. The mule refused to go, when Sergt. Ed. White gave him a tap with a stick. In less than two seconds the sergeant was sent flying through the air like a comet through space. "Blacky," an expert in horseback riding, was the next victim. He mounted, and as the mule began jumping and whirling he threw Blacky, but not quite so easily as the sergeant The mule was beginning to attract some attention

Corporal Tritapoe rushed into the arena with the remark, "Let me show you fellows how to ride that mule ; you don't know anything about mules " The corporal was a most excellent rider and tough as a pine knot. The boys gathered around enjoying the fun, with the remark, "I'll bet my old shoes that the corporal rides that mule." The corporal mounted, and the mule began tossing like a ship in a storm. The corporal endeavored to "hold the fort" by driving his spurs into the mule's ribs The effect was magical The mule kicked and jumped, and finally threw the corporal about 15 feet in the air, and he came near falling on the roof of a corn crib

This seemed to demonstrate beyond a shadow of a doubt that the aforesaid mule "was not built for cavalry"

The command moved on, leading a very quiet mule to camp. Sunday morning, May 16, Capt. Keyes, with 30 men, crossed the river at the Point of Rocks, on the ferry boat, the river being too high to ford, and started to Leesburg. As we passed the Big Spring a part of Mosby's command was attacked. Capts. Keyes and Grubb led the charge, and after a brisk encounter the enemy was routed, retreating in the direction of Leesburg. We captured three prisoners in the charge.

Sergt. James H. Beatty's fine bay horse, "Milroy," was badly shot in the leg and left on the field, and Sergt. Beatty picked up the first old plug he came to and followed the command

We passed through Leesburg and on to Waterford. We learned that the river had swollen so that the ferry boat could not cross with safety We passed through Hillsboro and on to Harpers Ferry, where we found the pontoon bridge washed away, and we sent the prisoners over in a skiff, and started back by way of Neersville.

On entering Hillsboro we ran into quite a squad of Mosby's men We struck them hard, capturing four prisoners. Company B had a horse shot. The prisoners were sent back to Harpers Ferry, taking them over the river in a skiff Then we pushed on down the valley, through Morrisonville and Wheatland, on to good old Waterford, where the Rangers were always made welcome We arrived after dark, going into camp at the home of Sergt. Dave Hough. The boys had a good supper on milk and sausage, and climbed up in the hay mow where all, except the pickets, enjoyed a first-class snooze for the night.

Monday morning, May 17, the command went into Waterford for breakfast. While the company was somewhat scattered, getting something to eat, our pickets were attacked by about 150 of Mosby's men. The pickets on the Hamilton Road were decoyed into a trap, killing Mike Ryan and James Monegan, of Company A, and dangerously wounding Sergt. Charles Stewart, of Company B.

Sergt. Stewart had four bullets through his body He was taken to Rachel Steers, a kind Quaker lady, who nursed him back to life. Dr. Bond kindly dressed his wounds twice a day until he recovered. The venerable doctor said his only ambition in life was to live long enough to make another hell for the man that shot Stewart after he surrendered.

Capt Keyes hurriedly formed his little band on a hill north of the town, where he received the onslaught of the enemy. We had to fire and fall back, fighting in this manner for about three miles, and in this engagement we lost five prisoners, viz , William Bull, John Ambrose, Peter Doherty, Henry Fouch, and Sergt James H. Beatty

We made a final stand about three miles from Waterford, but the enemy did not attack again

We had several horses shot, principally of Company B. We believe that company had two men slightly wounded, also

Those of our boys that were made prisoners were marched back through Waterford. Miss ———, one of the many loyal ladies of that burg, and perhaps the most demonstrative, kissed Sergt. James H Beatty, which made the mouths of Mosby's men water, but it was to no avail, as Miss ——— was a little particular who she kissed.

The prisoners were marched on through Hamilton and Upperville. That night, near Piedmont Station, Sergt. James H Beatty made a break for liberty. He darted through the woods in the darkness like a greyhound. About a hundred shots were fired after him, but he went faster than the bullets It was less then two months since he returned from Belle Isle Prison, that " hell on earth " The thoughts of so soon returning nerved him to outrun greased lightning. He traveled all night and part of the next day, and the next night arrived at Waterford, greatly to the delight of his friends He repaid Miss ——— with double compound interest, the kiss she so ungrudgingly bestowed thirty-six hours before. It was a clear case on Miss ———'s part of casting "bread upon the waters "

June 17 Mosby's men went to the residence of Sydnah Williams, near Taylortown, taking two loads of corn and then setting fire to his barn, wheat and hay stacks. The flames spread to the dwelling-house, entirely consuming all the buildings on the place. They also took Mr. C F Myers' horse and wagon, the worthy mail carrier between Point of Rocks and Waterford, while on his way home from the Point of Rocks.

During the early summer the rebels made numerous raids into the German and Quaker settlements for the purpose of collecting grain and supplies for that army

June 10, Capt Keyes with 30 men (of A and B) crossed the Potomac at Heater's Island, going direct to Waterford, where 40 of Mosby's men had passed about two hours before, going in the direction of Wheatland, with fifteen teams loaded with corn taken from the Union people of Loudoun. Capts. Keyes and Grubb marched their men directly to the Moore farm, near

Sergt. JAMES H. BEATTY, Co. A.

Corp HENRY C. HAUGH, Co. A.

Wheatland, where Mosby's men were to congregate and take the teams all together South under an escort.   It had been raining all day.   Our boys had put their gum blankets over them, completely hiding their uniforms. As we approached their meeting place ten teams, with an escort of Mosby's men, were approaching slowly   We let the wagons pass until the last one came up, the Johnnies behind it, when all parties halted, with a "Good evening," and began inquiring about the balance of the men.   At a given signal our boys pushed drawn revolvers in the faces of our friends " the enemy," and captured the entire lot without firing a shot.   The teams were turned out the pike towards Lovettsville.

Near the residence of Gen Wright we struck another squad, capturing two rebels and four more teams loaded with corn.

After passing Bolington, we encountered another lot of rebels and teams loaded, capturing four more prisoners   It was now dark.

We went to Lovettsville and on to Brunswick.   All the teams were sent back to their homes intact, much to the joy of the drivers   During the day we captured about 15 or 18 prisoners and about 20 splendid horses George H Harper's dun horse was in the lot.   Amongst the prisoners was one woman, traveling with Mosby's men.   Some women are very easy to please.   Much credit of the day's work is due to Sergt. Ed. White, Sergt. James H Beatty, Mahlon Best, George H. Harper, John Forsythe, George Hickman, Samuel Tritapoe, Joseph Fry, Joseph Ritchie, John Densmore, Flemon Anderson, and Joseph T. Divine.

A few days afterwards a squad was sent to Loudoun to look after Mosby's men that were again taking corn from Union citizens for the Confederacy.   When our boys arrived at Waterford they learned that some of Mosby's men had an appointment at James Walker's farm that

R—9

night to take a load of his corn. Our boys concealed themselves near the farm and awaited developments Mosby's men soon appeared from the direction of the mountains. When near the barn our squad attacked them, killing one (B. F. Barton) and capturing two others, and saved Mr Walker his corn.

The rebels were not contented by taking grain and teams from Union citizens, but would, with slight provocation, take the citizens as well. On one occasion three young men of Waterford, Charles Hollingsworth, Frank Rinker, and, we believe, Mr. Hough, while out sleighing, were captured with their teams and taken to near the Blue Ridge and released and allowed to walk back home.

On one occasion a detachment of Col White's men entered Waterford, claiming to have an order from the Confederate authorities for the arrest of Asa Bond, William Williams, and Robert Hollingsworth, three prominent Union citizens (Quakers) If any such an order had ever been issued it had been lost and one trumped up in its place. This order for their arrest was presented by James Mock and three other rebels. The spelling was a regular give-a-way—"acy bond bil Williams bob Hollinsworth." Mrs. Capt. Means and her sister, Miss Laura Bond, were absent, and on returning found the rebels at their father's, Asa Bond, claiming to have come to arrest Mr Bond and others, to be taken to Richmond and held as hostages for Henry Ball and others, who were confined at Fort McHenry, Baltimore. These bravehearted women opened a savage attack on the rebels with broomsticks, rollingpins, and clubs—woman's favorite weapons. Mrs Means ran to her residence, a few yards distant, rang the large bell, got her revolver, and fired two shots, when the terrified rebels fled in confusion These plucky women saved their father a trip to Richmond, and perhaps his life.

The same fellows, however, arrested William Williams and Robert Hollingsworth, taking them to Richmond, where they were confined in Libby Prison for
several months. The physical systems of both of these
gentlemen soon gave way under the barbarous treatment they received. By the intervention of the Quaker
citizens of Richmond both were transferred to private
prisons By the kind attention of Miss Van Lew, a
Quakeress, whom President Grant afterwards made
postmistress of Richmond, both gentlemen were made
comfortable until exchanged

CHAPTER X.

The Confederate Army under Gen Early Invades Mary-land—Battle of Monocacy—Frederick—Relay House—Ellicotts Mills—Washington

At this period of the war Gen. Grant was slowly but
surely fastening his iron grip on the throat of the Confederacy. It was only a question of time when the entire fabric would crumble beneath the mighty sledge
hammer that was raised to deliver the final blow.

The way of diverting the oncoming disaster that
seemed the most plausible to Gen Lee, was to have the
Federal army withdrawn from around Petersburg and
Richmond The way sought to accomplish this purpose was to send an invading army into Maryland and
attack Washington from the north The Confederacy
had also a secondary object to accomplish by this move,
that of gathering supplies for its army. A somewhat
erratic move by the Army of West Virginia also invited
the Confederates' third and last invasion of Maryland.

Gen. Hunter marched up the Shenandoah Valley with
considerable enthusiasm and even success, until he arrived before Lynchburg, where he found himself with-

out ammunition and rations, and over 200 miles from
his base of supplies.   By the aid of railroads the enemy
threw a formidable force in his front and rear, making
it impossible for him to return by the route he came.
He was compelled to cross the mountains and retire by
way of the Kanawha Valley to the Ohio River   This
movement on his part entirely withdrew all Federal
troops from the Valley, leaving it clear for the Confederates to march down into Maryland.   To Gen. Jubal
A Early was intrusted the mission of carrying out the
plan   He marched rapidly down the Valley to the Potomac   Gen. Franz Sigel, with a few hundred men, was
stationed at Martinsburg, guarding the Baltimore and
Ohio Railroad, keeping open communication with the
West.   He was not able to cope with the force of the
enemy, but fell back into Maryland   Gen. Max Weber,
in command at Harpers Ferry, withdrew to Maryland
Heights

Gen. Early's army of 25,000 men, formed into four
divisions, commanded by Gens Rhodes, Remseur,
McCausland, and Bradley T. Johnson, crossed the Potomac at Williamsport and at Shepherdstown July 3.

July 4 Col. Mosby's command of 400 men, with three
pieces of artillery, attacked our camp at Point of Rocks,
Md.   The artillery was stationed on the Virginia side of
the Potomac.   The attack began about 2 o'clock p m., by
the enemy throwing shells into our camp, while a large
body of cavalry crossed the river below Brunswick and
came down the towpath to the Point.   The enemy's
infantry was posted on a small island below the bridge,
to make it possible for their cavalry to cross the canal
and enter the village.

The place was garrisoned by two companies of the
1st Maryland P. H B (Capts. Bamford and Hardesty),
and Companies A and B, Loudoun Rangers, in command of Capts. Keyes and Grubb, making, all told,

about 225 men.   As we had no artillery, our forces fell
back beyond the range of their guns and formed in line
of battle, but the enemy entered the village, plundering
stores and railroad trains, which seemed to be their
principal mission on this raid.   Their troops, stationed
on the island, kept up a promiscuous firing into the
Point, one shot striking Miss Hester Ellen Fisher, a
young lady, while standing on her porch, killing her
instantly.   Our command sustained but slight loss from
this raid.   Capt Keyes was shot in the foot and one horse
killed   That evening our forces fell back to Frederick,
where Gen Tyler was in command with about 1,200
troops, and for the next two weeks the Rangers were
under fire every day.

July 5 Gen. Early's army occupied Hagerstown, Md.,
where they demanded $20,000 from the citizens, with
the threat that the town should be burned if the money
was not produced   The money was raised and their
city spared.

July 6 Boonsboro, Md., was visited by the Confederates   They obtained $20,000 from the citizens by
the same methods that were employed at Hagerstown.

July 7 the enemy visited Middletown, where they
also demanded $20,000.   The citizens asked for time to
consider this extraordinary demand.   The enemy refused time to consider the demand, but allowed the
citizens four hours to raise the money.   While the citizens were going down in their pockets for the cash the
rebel cavalry was riding through the streets singing,
"Maryland, My Maryland."   The words of the first
verse would almost bring blood out of a turnip—

> " The despot's heel is on thy shore,
>   Maryland, my Maryland,
> His torch is at thy temple's door,
>   Maryland, my Maryland "

This music evidently grated harshly on the ears of the Middletowners

July 7 Maj Yelliott, 1st Maryland P. H. B , with three companies of that regiment, and Companies A and B of the Loudoun Rangers, left Frederick, Md., about 7 o'clock, going in the direction of Middletown, to reconnoiter the position of the enemy. We marched until about 1 o'clock a. m., halting for the night on Catoctin Mountain, near Solomon's Gap At early dawn we found the rebel pickets stationed near where we rested for the night. The enemy had telegraph lines stretched across the pike in several places We cut them down, and advanced to near Middletown, where we struck a body of cavalry Maj. Yelliott ordered Corporal George V Kern and Robert Zee to advance about 300 yards to draw the fire of the enemy, which was returned by Kern and Zee. The enemy advanced within 50 yards of our line, when Capt. Grubb ordered a charge, driving them pell-mell into Middletown, where we ran into a brigade of Early's army. We fell back in good order While the enemy's bullets produced a tornado over our heads, we had but one man wounded—Isaac S Hough was shot in the arm and leg. Two men of Company B were also wounded, and several horses wounded The enemy formed in line of battle to meet an attack They supposed we were the advance of the Federal Army that had come to dispute their invasion We fell back to Solomon's Gap, where we met the 8th Illinois Cavalry and Alexander's Battery of 6 guns. The enemy advanced in force. Our forces made considerable noise to impress the enemy that there was a large army in their front. The ruse worked well. The enemy could have marched into Frederick City in three hours, whereas we kept them out for forty-eight hours.

The enemy advanced cautiously ; our battery would

throw a few shells into their advancing columns, which
caused them to slack up.   A courier was sent into Frederick to inform Gen Tyler of the situation.   Col. Gilpin,
of the 3d Maryland, was sent out, which brought our
force up to about 1,100 men.   Our forces had fallen
back until we were within five miles of Frederick.
Here a splendid position suggested a check of the
enemy.   We held the position until nearly dark, when
Col. Gilpin ordered a charge.   Alexander's boys turned
their artillery loose on the Johnnies.   Our infantry advanced and drove the rebels back to Catoctin Mountain.
After nightfall our forces withdrew to Frederick.   Col
Gilpin's loss during the day was about 12 killed and 50
wounded.   The loss of the enemy was about the same
     It was learned that night that the enemy was concen-
trating at Monocacy Junction.   Gen Tyler ordered the
entire garrison to put themselves in marching condition.
The streets of Frederick presented a scene of great ac-
tivity and some confusion.   It was known to both soldiers and citizens that a large Confederate army was
camped within 10 miles of the city, and that a battle was
inevitable in probably less than 24 hours, and possibly
in their own beautiful city   Gen. Tyler's troops moved
out on the Baltimore pike, about 9 o'clock p. m., crossing the stone bridge over the Monocacy River and turning sharply to the right, continued down the stream to
the Junction   The movement was made as quietly as
possible, and, of necessity, was tedious.   Several stops
were made during the night, so the infantry and trains
would be well up   We arrived about 1 o'clock a. m.,
and lay down on the ground, holding our horses by their
bridles.   We had been under fire for six days and nights,
and as soon as we struck the ground were sound asleep.
The sun rose clear and beautiful on the morning of the
9th.   Looking west across Monocacy River, about one
mile distant, lay Early's army, having arrived during

the night.   It was now settled beyond a doubt—both armies were encamped on ground where was to be fought a battle

Gen Lew Wallace arrived from Baltimore the day before with a few recruits and took command in person. Gen. Ricketts followed with the first and second brigades of the Third Division, Sixth Corps, making Gen Wallace's entire strength about 5,500 men of all arms. We had our light field battery (Alexander's), six guns, and two 20-pound siege guns   The latter were in the fort near the railroad bridge, and manned by a detachment of the 8th New York Heavy Artillery.

Gen. Lew Wallace made disposition for battle as follows.   His army occupying the eastern bank of the stream, while the enemy lay on the western bank of the same stream.   The river was about 50 yards wide, and contained about three to four feet of water.   The railroad bridge was in our immediate front ; the public bridge about 500 yards below the railroad bridge, at the crossing of the Washington turnpike ; the stone bridge about one mile above the railroad bridge, at the crossing of the Baltimore turnpike.   Gen Tyler was on the right with portions of Ohio and Maryland troops. Col Brown, with 149th Ohio, was stationed at the stone bridge, with instructions to hold it at all hazards. Gen. Ricketts, with the Sixth Corps troops, on the left, consisting of parts of 14th New Jersey, 87th Pennsylvania, 106th New York, 138th Pennsylvania, 110th, 122d, 126th Ohio, and three pieces of Alexander's Battery.   Gen. Lew Wallace in centre, with headquarters near railroad bridge, with the following troops : 151st New York, 10th Vermont, parts of 149th and 159th Ohio, 9th New York Heavy Artillery as infantry, and three pieces of Alexander's Battery, and two guns of the 8th New York Heavy Artillery.   In addition to this, Col Clendenin, 8th Illinois Cavalry, 400 men, and Lou-

Joseph T. Ritchie, Co. A.

Capt. James W. Virts, Co. D.

doun Rangers, two companies, about 80 men   The battle was opened by artillery.   The enemy began by
shelling our troops stationed near the railroad bridge.

Their sharpshooters took position in a large barn on
the west side of the stream, belonging to Mr Best.   A
few well-directed shots from our artillery set the barn
on fire, with several wheat and hay stacks, burning the
premises and compelling the enemy to seek other quarters.   Our skirmish line was thrown across the stream,
and advanced through a cornfield.   This brought on a
general engagement, which lasted until about 11
o'clock, when our line became heavily pressed and fell
back to near the bridge on the Baltimore pike.

The enemy made a determined effort to cross at this
point, but was repulsed   The fighting was so stubborn
that the water below the bridge was a crimson color
from the blood of the dead and wounded, of both armies,
that fell there.   The fighting now became general all
along the line   The enemy's artillery, eighteen pieces,
in a commanding position, kept up a constant cannonading on our line, particularly after 1 o'clock, which
was to cover the final assault that was soon to be made.
About 3 o'clock the enemy, with 12,000 troops with
two batteries, crossed the river two miles below the railroad bridge, and advanced against Ricketts' left with four
heavy columns, completely crushing it.   The fighting
at this final assault was excessively heavy and destruc-
tive on both sides   Our men held their ground to the
last, and were literally run over and trampled under foot
by superior numbers.   Our broken lines fell back six
miles to New Market, where they remained for the
night   The 6th Maryland and the 67th Pennsylvania
did not arrive until about 5 o'clock, and joined the
army there.

Our losses during the day were, killed, 102; wounded,
650, and 1300 prisoners.   The enemy's loss is reported

at 400   The New Jersey, New York, Pennsylvania and
Ohio troops lost heavily.   Probably the greatest loss fell
on the 14th New Jersey.   Every officer, both staff and
line, was either killed or wounded.   Of the 350 men

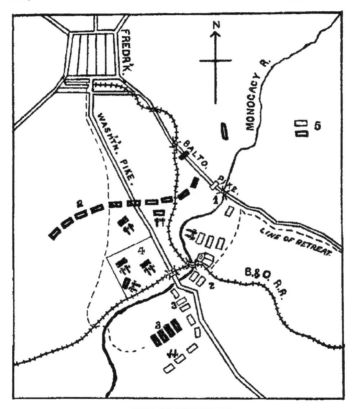

MAP OF MONOCACY
Light lines, Union , heavy lines, Confederate.

present 250 were either killed, wounded or prisoners,
but 95 reported for duty the next day.   As our men fell
back across the river they burned the bridge at the
Washington pike crossing   While the enemy was mak-

ing the final assault, their cavalry endeavored to gain our rear, but was unsuccessful. Our cavalry, under Col Clendenin, repelled their final assault, capturing the colors of the 17th Virginia Cavalry near Urbana.

Gen Lew Wallace made a patriotic stand. He did not entertain a belief of winning in a contest with an enemy whose numbers were six times greater than his own. He fought simply to gain time, and abundantly accomplished that object by detaining the enemy forty-six hours on their march to the Capital of the Nation—just the time required for the balance of the Sixth and the Nineteenth Corps to arrive from City Point. The positions occupied by the Rangers during the fight were : first, near the railroad bridge from there to the wagon bridge on the Washington pike, then guarding a ferry beyond Ricketts' left, then in support of three pieces of Alexander's Battery on Ricketts' left.

The day after the battle, July 10, the Confederates went back to their old tricks, they fleeced the City of Frederick out of $200,000 in cash by the same methods as were employed on other Maryland cities the week before.

July 10 Gen. Lew Wallace's army fell back in the defense of Washington and Baltimore, the Loudoun Rangers camping at Ellicotts Mills. The Baltimore and Ohio Railroad was an important factor in this campaign, as will be seen from the letter from Gen. Lew Wallace to John W. Garrett

"HEADQUARTERS MIDDLE DEPARTMENT,
"*Baltimore, Md , July 18, 1864*
"Hon JOHN W. GARRETT,
"*President Baltimore and Ohio Railroad*

"DEAR SIR : I avail myself of the first leisure moment to express to you and Mr. W. P. Smith my most sincere acknowledgment for the very great service rendered to me and my little army before and after the battle of Monocacy To sum it all up in a few words, I say frankly, that without your road, under your energetic and zealous management, it would have been impossible for me to have maintained my position for five minutes in the presence of the force that attacked me on that occasion.   Therefore, please accept my thanks and believe me, most truly and gratefully, your friend and servant

" LEW WALLACE,

" *Maj. Gen , Com'dg Eighth Army Corps,*
" *Middle Department.*"

The army marched direct on Washington, arriving in front of Fort Stevens, on the Seventh Street Road, late on the evening of July 11.   That night the balance of the Sixth and the Nineteenth Corps arrived on transports at the Seventh Street Wharf and marched direct to Fort Stevens.   At the break of day, July 12, Gen Early was preparing an assault on the Capital, when he discovered the slopes in his front covered with dense lines of blue.   The Sixth and Nineteenth Corps' skirmish lines were thrown out

Both sides were comparatively quiet until after four o'clock p. m., when the Sixth Corps attacked the enemy, driving them back two miles.   In this attack there was killed and wounded on each side about 300 men—the enemy losing 200 prisoners

Gen. Early now began to retreat, and the next day crossed the Potomac at Edward's Ferry (Leesburg) with his booty, consisting of nearly half a million in cash, nearly 3,000 head of cattle, and large quantities of merchandise taken from stores and warehouses.   The cash was principally obtained by levying contributions on towns as they passed through.   It was the old highwayman method of making a raise   With weapon in hand he attacks his unsuspecting victim, with the threat, " Your money or your life "

The Legislature of Maryland estimated that this raid cost the State over $2,000,000.

Conspicuous characters on this raid of burning and pillaging were two Marylanders, Gen. Bradley T. Johnson, of Frederick, and Maj. Harry Gilmore. They claimed to be fighting for their homes, while trying to destroy the State in which they were born and educated.

Ten days later, July 30, Gen McCausland, with Bradley T. Johnson and Harry Gilmore, crossed the Potomac with a brigade of cavalry near Williamsport Going direct to Pennsylvania, at Chambersburg, they demanded $100,000 in gold or $500,000 in greenbacks. The money was not produced, and the torch was applied and the beautiful city burned. Over 200 houses were destroyed and 1,500 persons rendered homeless.

The Sixth and Nineteenth Corps, under Gen Wright, followed Early through Leesburg to Snicker's Gap, where a battle was fought, about one hundred being killed on each side. Gen. Wright pushed on into the Shenandoah Valley In the meantime the Rangers moved up the Potomac, establishing camp at the Brick church, one mile north of Point of Rocks

A few days afterwards a squad of the Rangers crossed the Potomac, going to Leesburg, where we found some of White's men As we charged into town they fled south, going out the Dry Mill road We captured two prisoners, Ed Wright being one. We also captured several of their horses, including a beautiful small gray mare, a rapid pacer This handsome animal had been taken by Early's men from a citizen of Montgomery County, Maryland, a few weeks previous, on the recent raid.

August 19 a squad of the Rangers was sent to Loudoun, in command of Lieut. Atwell, to look after John Moberly, a notorious guerrilla. He belonged to White's command, but had assumed more the character of a bandit. He was annoying the citizens of Loudoun County almost beyond endurance. We crossed the Potomac at Mock's

Ford, going to near Leesburg, crossed the mountain at Gray's Gap. We learned that Moberly and 20 men were at Waterford, taking horses from everybody that possessed them, both Union and Secessionist We arrived there about 12 o'clock noon. A colored man had just come in on the Taylorstown road, bringing the information that Moberly and his gang were at the farm of Charles James, getting their dinners and their horses fed Lieutenant Atwell endeavored to capture the entire band by dividing his command into two squads, one to go out the Taylorstown road and enter the James farm from that road, while the other squad was to go through the Alder farm, "Scotland," and enter the James farm from the south, thus cutting off their retreat to the mountain As the first squad was entering from the Taylorstown road Moberly and his men had mounted and were preparing to leave. They halted and apparently prepared for a fight. By a premature discharge of Bill Hardy's carbine, who was in the second squad, and fully half a mile away, Moberly was made aware that he was about to be trapped, and his gang dashed away to the mountain before either of our squads had arrived near enough to make his capture sure The only hope now remaining was to overtake him before he got to the woods. In the chase we captured four prisoners and wounded Moberly in the arm We captured all but three of their horses.

When Moberly and his gang arrived at the mountain they dismounted and escaped in the thick underbrush, where our cavalry could not follow. The only casualty we had was Sergt. J. N Johnson's horse falling, painfully injuring him.

We recrossed the Potomac at Heater's Island. That night we guarded our prisoners in the Brick church, probably the first time they were ever in a church. The next day the prisoners were sent to Fort McHenry.

The boys seemed to enjoy our camp in this church more than they did in some other churches we had camped in.   They also endeavored to exercise a decorum that was appropriate to the place , the only exceptions being when some one put bumble bees in Sam Fry's bed, and when Joe Ritchie and Dr. Lenhart got into a fisticuff about a saddle blanket.

In obedience to orders from Gen. Stevenson at Harpers Ferry, Lieut. Atwell in command crossed the Potomac near Point of Rocks, Sunday morning, August 21, with 38 men of Companies A and B, on a raid to Aldie At Leesburg a squad of White's and the 1st Virginia Cavalry was encountered and routed.   Three of the enemy were captured, and all being badly wounded they were paroled and left at Leesburg, where one of them, Edwin Drish, died several days later.

The command continued by Dry Hollow and Grove Meeting House, near the latter place.   While marching through a strip of woods, a man was noticed sitting on the fence, holding his horse by the bridle rein, evidently waiting for the command to pass.

Lieut. Atwell rode up and began to question him. The fact was soon developed that he was a rebel quartermaster, by the name of Balthrop.   He was collecting supplies for that army   In his possession was found valuable papers   In a pair of saddle pockets attached to his saddle was found $200 in specie, $700 in greenbacks, and $2,000 in Confederate money   One of the Rangers recognized him as belonging to Ashby's Cavalry, while camped along the Potomac early in 1861, as quartermaster.

Passing on about two miles our advance guard ran into a squad of Mosby's men.   We drove them through Hamilton at a lively gait.   This same gang ran across a paroled Union soldier east of Hamilton early in the day and wilfully and maliciously murdered him.   He

told some of the citizens that he was on his way home
to the North.　He was buried near where he was killed,
in a piece of woods east of the village, about 50 yards
north of the pike.　If we had caught any of Mosby's
men that day it would have gone roughly with them
on account of murdering this defenceless soldier.　A
small board was planted at the head of his grave, bearing these melancholy words:

"Unknown Union Soldier"

No doubt some fond mother has waited tidings of her
boy for lo, these many years　Our prisoner was turned
over to headquarters, with his money, at Harpers Ferry.

CHAPTER XI

Gen. Sheridan in the Valley—Battles of Winchester, Fisher's Hill, Tom's Brook, Cedar Creek

The frequency of the Confederate raids into Maryland and Pennsylvania had been a source of great annoyance to the authorities at Washington, as by them
the army of the enemy was largely supplied with forage.
Every recurrence of these raids gave them that much
longer lease on life.　Another aspect of the case which
perhaps was not as far-reaching in results, though
equally as annoying—the loyal citizens of Maryland
and Pennsylvania had bitterly complained of their
houses and barns being plundered and burned, and
their accumulations of years entirely swept away by
the enemy

After the pillaging and burning of Chambersburg,
Pa, July 30, 1864, by the enemy, the War Department
took decisive steps to stop these raids　Gen. Grant
took the matter in hand.　First, the Shenandoah Valley
should be completely canceled from the theatre of war.
The mountains that flanked it made it a sure pathway

Lieut. AUGUSTUS C. RHODES, Co B.

Sergt. GEORGE H. C. HICKMAN, Co. B.

down which the Confederates could be sent at almost any time to invade the North, while the fertile fields largely contributed to the feeding of that army. It was an important work, and great care should be exercised in the selection of a commander to carry it to a successful termination

Gen. Hunter was in command of the Department and was satisfactory to Gen Grant, but owing to a lack of harmony between Gen. Halleck and Gen. Hunter, the latter, at his own request, was relieved from this command. Gen. Grant now selected Gen. Phil. Sheridan, who met with some slight objection from the War Department, as Secretary Stanton thought he was rather young (thirty-three years) for a command so important It is alleged that Gen Halleck objected on account of "Bad grammar," as he termed it, as Sheridan had a kind of "Wild West" style of giving orders, using such expressions as "Licked them out of their boots;" "Hammered the stuffing out of them," etc. Such expressions seemed to grate harshly on the cultured ear of Gen Halleck.

President Lincoln said he did not know that grammar cut much of a figure in fighting, as he remembered the worst licking he ever got was from a lad who did not know the alphabet, and if grammar was the only objection he thought it safe to try Sheridan.

Phil. H. Sheridan had not been a Cicero at West Point, standing thirty-four in a class of fifty-two. He had also been suspended for one year for quarreling with his tutor. Gen Grant's judgment in the selection of a subordinate had never failed him, and in this case he was allowed full sway, and Gen. Sheridan was appointed August 7, as Commander of the Army of the Shenandoah.

Subsequent events practically demonstrated that the selection was wise—an excellent strategist of rare mili-

R—10

tary judgment, a brave and aggressive fighter, and a well-poised commander

The instructions originally prepared for Gen. Hunter were transferred to Gen. Sheridan, as follows :

"On pushing up the Shenandoah Valley, where it is expected you will have to go first, or last, it is desirable that nothing should be left to invite the enemy to return. Take all provisions, forage, and stock wanted for the use of your command, and such as can not be consumed, destroy It is not desirable that the buildings should be destroyed ; they should rather be protected , but the people should be informed that so long as an army can subsist amongst them recurrences of these raids must be expected, and we are determined to stop them at all hazards. * * * Make your own arrangements for supplies of all kinds, giving regular vouchers for such as will be taken from loyal citizens in the country through which you march.

"Very respectfully,

"U. S. GRANT,
"*Lieutenant General.*"

"HEADQUARTERS MIDDLE DEPARTMENT,
"*Baltimore, Md., July 18, 1864*

"Brig. Gen. E B TYLER, U S. Volunteers,
"*Comd. First Separate Brigade.*

"GENERAL : I am directed by Maj Gen Wallace to request you to return the Loudoun Rangers (Virginia Cavalry) to Harpers Ferry, and to report to Maj Gen Hunter

"I am, very respectfully, your obedient servant,
"SAMUEL B LAWRENCE,
"*Lieut. Col. and Asst. Agt. General.*"

In obedience to the above orders, the Rangers moved with the rest of the brigade, and took position on the left, camping on a steep hillside overlooking the Shenandoah River.

The Army of the Shenandoah was camped from Harpers Ferry to Halltown, and composed of the following troops

The Sixth Corps, commanded by Gen Wright ,

The Nineteenth Corps, commanded Gen Emory ;

The 8th Corps (known also as the Army of West Virginia), commanded by Gen Crook.

Gen. Sheridan put the army in motion, moving up the valley to Strasburg, where Gen. Early had received reinforcements and attacked our forces. Gen. Sheridan had not become sufficiently acquainted with his army and the country to justify him in measuring steel with the enemy, consequently he fell back to Halltown, where the greater portion of his army remained for several weeks. So far the campaign had been on the defensive. There had been skirmishing every day, principally by the cavalry.

Gen. Grant visited Sheridan at Halltown early in September, and was in thorough accord with the latter's plan of campaign, which from this time forward was to be aggressive. The cavalry now found plenty to do, as there was not a day, or an hour, but there was a ·clash of arms in that branch of the service. Several engagements rose to the dignity of a battle and àre worthy of mention : Front Royal, August 16; Winchester, the 17th ; Summit Point and Berryville, the 21st ; Halltown, the 24th ; Kearneysville, the 25th ; Halltown, the 26–27th ; Smithfield, the 29th , Berryville, September 3d–4th , Locks Ford, the 13th , Martinsburg, the 17th.

In these preliminary engagements our forces lost about 600 men, and the enemy's loss was about the same

Saturday, September 17, Gen. Early moved a large portion of his army to Martinsburg, threatening an invasion of Maryland, while the main portion of his army lay at Winchester and Bunker Hill. The bulk of our army lay near Berryville   Sheridan's opportunity had arrived and he knew it.   He put his army in motion at 4 o'clock a. m , September 19, in the direction of Winchester.   The cavalry, under Torbert and Wilson, opened the way by forcing the passage of Opequon Creek   There was but one good road, the Berryville pike, and the country hilly.   It was 10 o'clock before the troops had crossed the stream and got into position on the west side   This delay gave the enemy time to recall his two divisions from Martinsburg.

The Sixth and the Nineteenth Corps advanced under a heavy artillery fire.   Our line immediately became engaged, and fought with a desperation that has rarely been equalled   There was a total lack of earthworks, or protection of any kind, hence the fighting was desperate and bloody.   About 11 o'clock the enemy made a counter charge, striking our center, and forcing it back about a quarter of a mile.   Gen. Russell's division of the Sixth Corps was thrown against the new move of the enemy, and in turn drove him back and re-established our old line   Crook's Eighth Corps was still kept in reserve to be thrown on the left and south of Winchester to cut off retreat, but the heavy fighting on the right, by the Sixth and Nineteenth Corps, compelled a change of programme.

The Eighth Corps was hurriedly transferred to that point and attacked the enemy's left with such vigor as to double them back in a confused mass, from which they did not recover, but fled in confusion.   Simultaneously with this the Sixth and Nineteenth Corps were ordered forward.   At the same time the cavalry, Wilson on the left and Torbert on the right, charged, when their whole army fled through Winchester and on up the valley, panic stricken   Darkness alone saved Early's army from capture by our cavalry in the battle of the Opequon, or Winchester Gen. Sheridan lost 5,000 men. Gen. Early lost about 4,500.

The Sixth Corps lost. 1699 The Eighth Corps The Nineteenth lost . . . . . 800 Corps lost . 2074 The Cavalry Corps . lost 450

The enemy lost Genls. Goodwin and Rhodes, killed, with five guns and nine battle flags, and 1,500 prisoners Sheridan lost Gen, Russell of the Sixth Corps, killed. The following regiments lost heavily :

Sixth Corps

2d Connecticut Heavy   11th Vermont (1st
  Artillery 138   Heavy Artillery). . 99
37th Massachusetts In-
  fantry   . 91

Nineteenth Corps

114th New York In-   22d Iowa 105
  fantry   . . . 185   3d Massachusetts Dis-
12th Maine 112   mounted Cavalry. . 106
26th Massachusetts . 139   156th New York. . 111
14th New Hampshire 138

Eighth Corps.

34th Massachusetts . 102 91st Ohio 106
10th West Virginia . 97

Custer's Cavalry.

1st Michigan . . . . 39 6th Michigan . 20
5th Michigan . . . 24 7th Michigan 23

Lowell's Cavalry

2d Massachusetts. . 20 2d United States . . 29
1st United States . . 24 5th United States . . 29

McIntosh's Cavalry.

3d New Jersey . . . 21 18th Pennsylvania 20

The number of troops engaged on both sides was about equal. Early's army being on the defensive and on chosen ground gave him the advantage by fully 5,000 men.

While the battle was in progress Sheridan was constantly at the front infusing his troops with his powerful enthusiasm and valor

This victory of Sheridan's created unbounded enthusiasm throughout the North, and especially in Washington The imaginary doubt that lingered around the War Department, on account of age or " bad grammar," was entirely dispelled. President Lincoln's heart was so full of enthusiasm and approval of Sheridan's method of fighting that he wired him the following

" EXECUTIVE MANSION,

" *Washington, September 20, 1864*

" Maj.-Gen. SHERIDAN, *Winchester, Va.*

" Have just heard of your great victory   God bless you all, officers and men   Strongly inclined to come up and see you   " A LINCOLN "

" WAR DEPARTMENT,

" *Washington, September 20, 1864*

" Maj.-Gen SHERIDAN (in the field).

" Please accept for yourself and your gallant army the thanks of the President and this Department for your great battle and brilliant victory yesterday.   The President has appointed you a Brigadier-General in the Regular Army, and you have been assigned to the permanent command of the Middle Division.   One hundred guns were fired here at noon to-day in honor of your victory.

" EDWIN M. STANTON,

" *Secretary of War.*"

Sheridan's method of fighting was not to allow his antagonist time for recuperation, and by early dawn, September 20th, his army was in motion in pursuit of the enemy, who were overtaken at Fisher's Hill, an almost impregnable position, especially from the north. This is the narrowest point in the Valley, four miles from mountain to mountain. Gen Early had previously erected works of defence across the Valley, and on exceptionally high ground. Late in the afternoon Sheridan established a heavy skirmish line, and kept up firing until after dark. During the night the Eighth Corps was concealed in heavy timber on the extreme right in this obscure position during the 21st, while the Sixth and Nineteenth Corps were placed in the front center of the enemy's position, drawing a brisk fire from their line, which in turn was partly attacked by Ricketts' and Getty's divisions of the Sixth Corps (thus holding the close attention of the enemy), while Torbert, Wilson and Merritt, of the cavalry, were ordered through Luray Valley, to get in the enemy's rear near New Market.

During the night of the 21st the Eighth Corps was quietly moved into the timber at the foot of Little North Mountain, entirely obscured from view of the enemy. Ricketts' division of the Sixth Corps was moved with Averell's Cavalry to the right, and attacked the enemy's left, while Crook suddenly swung his corps out of the woods, and sprang upon the unsuspecting enemy's left and rear with the vigor of a tiger, throwing them into utter confusion and rout, and in quick succession the Sixth and Nineteenth Corps burst upon the Confederate centre, making the disaster complete. The cavalry under Torbert was detained by the enemy in Luray Valley, and did not arrive in time to co-operate with the infantry, thus leaving a gap for the fleeing enemy to escape

In the battle of Fisher's Hill, Gen Sheridan lost 500 men and the enemy lost 1,500, besides 15 pieces of artillery, a large portion of his wagon train and nearly all his tents.

The Sixth Corps lost	238	The Eighth Corps lost.	162
The Nineteenth Corps lost 114		The cavalry lost . . .	14

Sixth Corps regiments lost heavily—

2d Connecticut, heavy artillery	20	139th Pennsylvania. 126th Ohio.	26 32

Nineteenth Corps Regiments.

128th New York	 20

Eighth Corps Regiments.

34th Massachusetts	18	91st Ohio 16

Gen Early's report of this battle is vague, as usual. He says :

"Late yesterday the enemy attacked my position at Fisher's Hill and succeeded in driving back the left of my line, which was defended by cavalry, and throwing a force into the left of my infantry, when the whole of the troops gave way in a panic, and could not be rallied. This resulted in a loss of twelve pieces of artillery, though my loss in men is not large "

Sheridan followed up this victory by continuing after the enemy until after midnight For the next ten days our cavalry was continually on the heels of the enemy, capturing stragglers, trains, and supplies. On the 25th the infantry halted at Harrisonburg, while the cavalry proceeded on to Staunton, where large quantities of arms, ammunition and commissary stores was captured. All railroad bridges were burned and the rolling stock destroyed.

October 5th Sheridan began to move down the valley and to carry out the orders issued—"to leave the valley untenable for an army."

The infantry moved first with the wagon trains, while the cavalry formed across the entire valley, burning every particle of grain and forage that an army could subsist on. Every flour mill and grist mill, and everything that contributed to the aid or comfort of the Confederacy was destroyed. All live stock, horses, cattle, sheep, and hogs were taken. Gen. Early received reinforcements from Longstreet early in October, and his cavalry followed in the wake of Custer, keeping a few miles behind At Woodstock they attacked Custer's division, skirmishing as far as Toms Brook, where Sheridan halted the infantry one day and told his cavalry " they must whip the enemy or get whipped themselves."

October 9th Custer and Merritt's divisions turned back and attacked the enemy's forces of 5,000 men under Gens. Rosser, Lomax, and Bradley T Johnson, and after a short but stubborn engagement the enemy was disastrously defeated, with the loss of nearly 400 prisoners, all their artillery, eleven guns, and their entire trains—Sheridan said in his report " everything they had on wheels."

This was one of the most complete cavalry victories of the war. The enemy was driven 25 miles. Sheridan's loss was 9 killed and 48 wounded.

Gen Rosser's army was known as the Laurel division. Each person wore a bunch of laurel in his hat to typify great bravery.

A good story that grew out of this battle is told at the expense of Gen Rosser. Gen Imboden, who commanded a brigade in Early's army, had only been moderately successful as a commander, and Rosser never lost an opportunity to taunt Imboden about his record as a soldier. After this battle (Toms Brook) Imboden sent word to Rosser, asking how he would trade laurel for cannon.

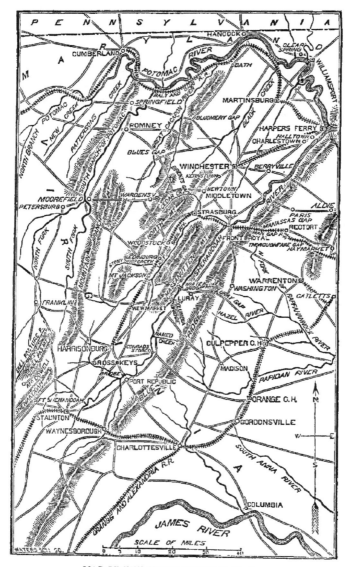

MAP OF THE SHENANDOAH VALLEY.

The Sixth Corps was ordered to return to the Army of the Potomac near Petersburg, while the cavalry continued its raid, making the Valley untenable for a crow without rations Sheridan's work in the Valley was apparently finished. A wish had been expressed from the War Department that Gen. Sheridan should establish a "base of supplies" near Manassas Gap, with a view of a further advance on Gordonsville and finally Richmond Sheridan opposed this scheme, not because he was opposed to supplies, but he could see no need of a "base " as long as there were rebels running around loose shooting at people. He was sent to the Valley to destroy "bases of supplies," and not to establish them. Finally this subject called him to Washington on the following telegram :

"WASHINGTON, D C , *October 13, 1864.*
" Maj Gen SHERIDAN.
"[Through Gen Augur.]
" If you can come here, a consultation on several points is extremely desirable. I propose to visit Gen. Grant, and would like to see you first.
"E. M. STANTON,
"*Secretary of War.*"

On Gen. Sheridan's arrival at Front Royal the 16th, he received the following from Gen. Wright at Cedar Creek :

" HEADQUARTERS MIDDLE MILITARY DIVISION.
" *October 16, 1864.*
"Maj. Gen. P. H SHERIDAN.
" I enclose you dispatch which explains itself. * * *
If the enemy should be strongly re-enforced by cavalry he might by turning our right give us a great deal of trouble I shall hold on here until the enemy's movements are developed and shall only fear an attack on my right, which I shall strongly resist.
"H. G. WRIGHT,
"*Maj. Gen Com'dg* "

"Lieut Gen EARLY.

  " Be ready to move as soon as my forces join you, and we will crush Sheridan.

" LONGSTREET,
" *Lieut. Gen* "

This message was taken from the rebel signal station on Three Top Mountain, and was thought at first to be a ruse, but other events had partly confirmed it. Sheridan therefore ordered his scattered forces concentrated at Cedar Creek.

"Maj Gen. H. G WRIGHT,
    " *Commanding Sixth Corps*

  " GENERAL : The cavalry is all ordered back to you. Make your position strong. If Longstreet's dispatch is true, he is under the impression that we have largely detached. I will go over to Augur, and may get additional news. Close in Col. Powell, who will be at this point. If the enemy should make an advance, I know you will defeat him. Look well to your ground, and be well prepared. Get up everything that can be spared I will bring up all I can, and will be up Tuesday if not sooner.

" P. H. SHERIDAN,
" *Maj. General.*"

Gen. Sheridan left for Washington, arriving at daylight the 17th After a conference at the War Department and the White House about two hours, he immediately left for Martinsburg. By the night of the 18th he was at Winchester on his return. Early next morning artillery could be heard up the Valley. As that was a daily occurrence no especial significance was attached to it

When Gen. Sheridan left for Washington he placed Gen. Wright in command of the army in his absence, which was encamped on the north bank of Cedar Creek— the Eighth Corps on the left, the Nineteenth Corps in center, and the Sixth Corps on the right rear. The enemy was encamped at Fisher's Hill. During the night of the 18th a Confederate force, under Gen. Gordon, crossed North Fork, passing between the mountain and the river, until below the junction of Cedar Creek, and recrossed at Bowman's Ford, striking the Eighth Corps in flank and rear, throwing them into disorder. This was immediately followed by Gen. Early with the remainder of his force crossing Cedar Creek and striking the Eighth and Nineteenth Corps in center, driving the whole line back in confusion. The enemy's line was moving northwest in the direction of the Valley pike, threatening our rear. The Sixth Corps lay one and a half miles to the right and rear of the Nineteenth Corps. By the time the enemy reached the line of the Sixth Corps the latter was formed and attacked the oncoming hosts of Early and temporarily checked them, but the stampede that so early set in could not be stopped. Gen. Wright ordered his troops to fall back to take better position Gen. Getty was ordered to cover the retreat. Gen. Wright made several stands with his troops, and partly succeeded in checking the pursuing enemy. During the early morning our army lost 18 guns and 1,300 prisoners.

About 8 30 o'clock, while Gen Sheridan was leaving Winchester, the distant roar of artillery convinced him that a battle was being fought. He had not proceeded more than one mile when the head of the column of fugitives came in sight Whereupon Sheridan thundered out—

" Face the other way and go back ¹ "

He ordered the two brigades at Winchester to form across the Valley and turn all stragglers back, while with an escort of twenty men he started at full speed for the front, riding his famous black horse " Winchester," arriving at the scene of action, near Middletown, at 11 o'clock, accompanied by three members of his escort,

the horses of the others having given out.   As he rode
up he delivered that short but inspiring oration that will
live as long as the Valley lasts :

"Face the other way, boys, we are going back to our
camp ; we are going to lick them out of their boots."

The return of Gen. Sheridan was magical.   As soon
as his presence was known a complete transformation
took place   Where a few minutes before doubt and uncertainty prevailed, now unbounded enthusiasm and
confidence was apparent everywhere   Sheridan made
some slight changes in his line of battle   Soon the
enemy came forward to attack, and was handsomely
repulsed.

It was reported that the enemy was moving a heavy
column north on the Front Royal pike, in the direction
of Winchester.   This rumor caused Gen. Sheridan to
defer an immediate advance on the enemy, but he soon
learned that no such movement was being made by the
enemy.   Every nerve was now bent on an immediate
attack

At 4 o'clock our entire line moved forward to the attack   The enemy, well protected behind stone fences,
gave some temporary trouble   The First Division of
the Nineteenth Corps (Gen. McMillan) made a gallant
charge, completely dislodging the enemy, and from this
time until night our troops swept everything before
them   Our invincible cavalry now fell upon both flank
and rear of the enemy, capturing cannon, trains and prisoners by the score.   The retreat of the enemy became
disorderly, and degenerated into a skedaddle.   The cavalry charge by Custer's Division was especially brilliant
and successful, forcing the passage of Cedar Creek, driving the terror stricken enemy beyond Strasburg, recapturing the 18 guns lost in the morning, and capturing
26 additional ones from the enemy.   Also 20 caissons,

30 wagons, 38 ambulances, over 300 horses and mules, 4,000 stand of arms and 1,500 prisoners.

There was little difference in the loss of the two armies Gen. Sheridan's loss was 5,500, including the 1,300 prisoners lost early in the morning and hurried off South. Gen. Early's loss was probably about the same as Sheridan's

Losses by Corps.

Sixth Corps	2,126	Provisional Division	102
Nineteenth Corps.	2,383	Cavalry	200
Eighth Corps . . .	860		

Regiments suffering heavy losses, were .

Sixth Corps.

2d Connecticut Heavy Artillery . . .	190	15th New Jersey Infantry. . .	85
9th New York Heavy Artillery . . .	208	102d Pennsylvania Infantry. . . .	92
11th Vermont (1st Heavy Artillery) .	107		

Eighth Corps.

5th New York Heavy Artillery	309	11th West Virginia Infantry.	77
23d Ohio Infantry. .	72		

Nineteenth Corps.

29th Maine Infantry .	127	12th Connecticut Infantry.	172
30th Massachusett's	108		
114th New York Infantry.	115	47th Pennsylvania Infantry.	154
8th Vermont Infantry	106		

Provisional Division.

6th New York Heavy Artillery	93

Cavalry.

1st Michigan . . .	28	2d Massachusetts .	24
7th Michigan . . .	35	2d New York . .	14

Our army lost four brigade commanders killed .

Gen. Bidwell, Sixth Corps

Col Thoburn, Eighth Corps.

Col. Lowell, Cavalry Corps.

Gen. Ketching, Provisional Division.

Gen. Early, in his report says " My loss in artillery was twenty-three pieces, some wagons and ambulances My loss in killed and wounded is less than one thousand. I can not say how many men were captured, but think very few."

This battle seems to have been much misunderstood. It has been stated by some competent writers that all the fighting was done by the Sixth Corps, while all the running was done by the Eighth and Nineteenth Corps.

That all retreated in the morning and all returned and fought in the evening is conclusively shown by an examination of Gen. Sheridan's and the Corps command's reports.

Gen Grant's army at Shiloh and Gen. Sheridan's army at Cedar Creek had identically the same experience, as both were surprised and defeated early in the fight, and both were victorious beyond measure at the close of the fight

Gen. Sheridan says

" I am pleased to be able to state that the strength of the Sixth and Nineteenth Corps and Crook's command was now (12 m.) being rapidly augmented by the return of those who had gone to the rear early in the day."

Gen Wright, Sixth Corps, says :

" I felt every confidence that the enemy could be promptly defeated. In this anticipation, however, I was sadly disappointed. Influenced by a panic, which often seizes the best of troops (and some of them I have seen behave admirably under the hottest fire), the line broke before the enemy came in sight, and under a scat-

BRISCOE GOODHART, Co. A.

tering fire retreated in disorder down the pike. * * *
Everything having been prepared and the men somewhat rested from the fatigue of the morning, an advance was ordered by Gen Sheridan of the entire line "

Gen. McMillan, Nineteenth Corps, says

" * * * Had there been concert of action through
our whole forces, I believe there was no time, after we
formed on the position of the Sixth Corps, that I could
not have driven the enemy in my front without difficulty. * * * When Gen. Sheridan made his ap-
pearance, he was most heartily cheered along the whole
line, so far as I could observe. The officers and men
seemed at once to recover from a kind of lethargy,
* * * and by the time the commanding general had
perfected his arrangements for attacking the enemy the
men were in as good mental condition to fight as at any
period when victory encouraged," etc.

The battle of Cedar Creek put the cap-stone on Sheridan's career as a soldier, making him the most gallant
and brilliant military hero of the day Sheridan's ride
from Winchester to Middletown is a living reality.
The American public never tires reading it.

R—11

GEN. SHERIDAN, AS HE APPEARED ON THIS RIDE.

SHERIDAN'S RIDE.

T. B. READ.

Up from the south at break of day,
Bringing to Winchester fresh dismay,
The affrighted air with a shudder bore,
Like a herald in haste to the chieftain's door,
The terrible grumble, and rumble, and roar,
Telling the battle was on once more,
And Sheridan twenty miles away.

And wider still those billows of war
Thundered along the horizon's bar,
And louder yet into Winchester rolled
The roar of that red sea uncontrolled,
Making the blood of the listener cold
As he thought of the stake in that fiery fray,
With Sheridan twenty miles away.

But there's a road from Winchester town,
A good broad highway leading down ,
And there, thro' the flash of the morning light,
A steed as black as the steeds of night
Was seen to pass as with eagle flight ,
As if he knew the terrible need,
He stretched away with the utmost speed ,
Hills rose and fell—but his heart was gay,
With, Sheridan fifteen miles away

Under his spurning feet the road
Like an arrowy Alpine river flowed,
And the landscape flowed away behind,
Like an ocean flying before the wind ,
And the steed like a bark fed with furnace-ire
Swept on with his wild eyes full of fire ;
But lo ! he is nearing his heart's desire,
He is snuffing the smoke of the roaring fray,
With Sheridan only five miles away

The first that the General saw were the groups
Of stragglers, and then the retreating troops ,
What was done—what to do—a glance told him both,
And, striking his spurs with a terrible oath,
He dashed down the line 'mid a storm of hurrahs,
And the wave of retreat checked its course there, because
The sight of the master compelled it to pause.
With foam and with dust the black charger was gray,
By the flash of his eye and his nostril's play
He seemed to the whole great army to say
"I have brought you Sheridan all the way
From Winchester town to save the day ! "

Hurrah ! hurrah ! for Sheridan !
Hurrah ! hurrah ! for horse and man !
And when their statues are placed on high,
Under the dome of the Union sky—
The American soldiers' temple of fame—
There with the glorious General's name,
Be it said, in letters both bold and bright
" Here is the steed that saved the day
By carrying Sheridan into the fight
From Winchester, twenty miles away ! "

President Lincoln, the War Department, and the American Congress vied with each other in honoring Sheridan, as the following will show :

          "Executive Mansion,
            " *Washington, October 22, 1864.*
" Maj. Gen. Sheridan.

"With great pleasure I tender to you and your brave army the thanks of the nation, and my own personal admiration and gratitude, for the month's operations in the Shenandoah Valley, and especially for the splendid work of October 19, 1864.

       " Your obedient servant,
            "Abraham Lincoln."

"War Department, Adjt. General's Office,
         " *Washington, November 14, 1864.*

      "[General Orders, No. 282.]

"Ordered by the President   *   *   *   2. That for the personal gallantry, military skill and just confidence in the courage and patriotism of his troops, displayed by Philip H. Sheridan on the 19th day of October, at Cedar Run, whereby, under the blessing of Providence, his routed army was reorganized, a great national disaster averted, and a brilliant victory achieved over the rebels for the third time in a pitched battle within thirty days, Philip H. Sheridan is appointed major general in the United States Army, to rank as such from the 8th day of November, 1864.

" By order of the President of the United States.
            "E. D. Townsend,
          " *Assistant Adjutant General.*"

       "[Public Resolution, No. 13.]

" *Be it resolved by the Senate and House of Representatives of the United States of America in Congress assembled,* That the thanks of Congress are hereby tendered to Major General Philip H. Sheridan, and the officers and men under his command, for the gallant military skill and courage displayed in the brilliant series of victories achieved by them in the Valley of the Shenandoah, and especially for their services at Cedar Creek on the 19th day of October, 1864, which retrieved the fortunes of the day and thus averted a great disaster.

SEC. 2. *And be it further resolved,* That the President of the United States be, and hereby is, requested to communicate this resolution to Major General Sheridan, and through him to the officers and soldiers under his command.

"Approved February 9, 1865.

"By order of the Secretary of War.

"E. D. TOWNSEND,
"Assistant Adjutant General."

The battle of Cedar Creek practically ended the campaign in the Valley. The enemy had been defeated and humiliated beyond measure The Valley, where their intrepid army had held undisputed sway for three long years, had now been wrested from them, and was the "dwelling place" of their enemies. The land that had fed and sheltered their armies now furnished them "bitter waters." In closing with the battle of Cedar Creek, we wish to impress upon the mind of the reader the "unfaltering" fidelity and patriotism of Phil Sheridan's famous black horse, "Winchester" Perhaps we can partly do him justice by relating the following incident :

Some years after the war an evangelist and great admirer of Sheridan was holding a revival in the blue grass region of Kentucky. Among the many that professed religion was Gen. Abe Buford, an ex-Confederate, a gentleman noted for owning a number of fine race horses , with his change of heart, his love for fine horses seemed to increase The evangelist called on the general a few days after his conversion, and the Kentuckian's heart overflowed with praises for fine horses, and he assured the revivalist that there would be horses in heaven. " Yes," said the good parson, "and the horse that Phil Sheridan rode from Winchester to Cedar Creek will have the front seat "

The fragments of Early's army, with the exception of small roving bands, were soon drawn towards Richmond, where the final battle was to be fought, while.Sheridan's cavalry completed the work of destruction in the Valley.'

In performing a mission of this kind, where the work of destruction was intrusted to so many hands, it would naturally be expected that many acts of lawlessness would be committed. There may have been some, but history fails to record a single case where private property was perverted to personal gain, or where tribute was demanded from any source.

NOVEMBER 24, 1864.
Maj. Gen. H. W. HALLECK, U S. Army,
Chief of Staff, Washington, D. C

GENERAL : I have the honor to transmit herewith a report of property captured and destroyed and lost by capture by the Middle Military Division during the campaign commencing August 10 and ending November 16, 1864, in accordance with telegraphic orders received from you.

I am, general, yours, respectfully,
P. H. SHERIDAN,
Major-General Commanding.

Report of property captured and destroyed (from the enemy) by the Middle Military Division, Maj. Gen P. H. Sheridan, commanding, during the campaign commencing August 10, 1864, and ending November 16, 1864

Pieces artillery .	94	Barns		1,200
Caissons	89	Furnaces		7
Limbers	8	Tanueries		4
Forges .	6	Railroad depot .		1
Battery Wagon	1	Locomotive .		1
Artillery ammuni-		Box cars		3
tion . rounds	23,000	Wheat	bushels	435,802
Army wagons	131	Oats	do .	20,000
Ambulances	137	Corn	do .	77,176
Medical wagons .	7	Flour	barrels	874
Harness sets	1,134	Hay	tons	20,397
Horse equipments do	1,140	Fodder	do	500
Battle flags	40	Straw	do	450
Small-arms	19,230	Beef cattle		10,918
Small-arm ammu-		Sheep		12,000
nition rounds	1,061,000	Swine		15,000
Horses	3,772	Calves		250
Mules .	545	Bacon and hams lbs		2,000
Flour mills	71	Tobacco	do	10,000
Woolen mill . .	1	Rails .	miles	947
Saw-mills	8	Potatoes	bushels	2,500
Powder mill	1	Cotton yarn	pounds	1,665
Saltpeter works	3			

November 28, Gen. Merritt and Col Crowninshield with two brigades of cavalry left Winchester on a raid into Loudoun and Fauquier counties, with orders to destroy all forage and supplies that the enemy could subsist on They captured 87 horses, 475 beef-cattle, and 100 sheep, and destroyed 230 barns, 8 mills, 1 still house, 10,000 tons of hay, and 25,000 bushels of grain.

Report of property lost by capture by the Middle Military Division during the campaign commencing August 10, 1864, and ending November 16, 1864

Pieces artillery	24	Medical wagons	2
Caissons	19	Harness. . . sets	726
Forges	16	Horse equipments do	525
Battery wagons .	3	Small-arms.	1,849
Artillery ammuni-		Small-arm ammu-	
tion . rounds	460	nition . . rounds	1,200
Army wagons	86	Horses . .	359
Ambulances	48	Mules . .	564

Most of the articles under the heading "lost by capture" 'were recaptured subsequently.   The twenty-four
pieces of artillery were all recaptured.

Sheridan's career in the valley accomplished a double
purpose, as he not only banished the enemy, but taught
our own Government a valuable lesson.

Some of the early prominent generals of the war,
and others that were high in authority, declared the
cavalry to be of little value in modern warfare, and
doubted if it could ever be made efficient.   Sheridan's
Valley campaign demonstrated beyond question that
when efficiently led the cavalry was the most valuable
arm of the service.

The greater portion of the Army of the Shenandoah
lay for about five weeks near Winchester, enjoying a
brief respite.   December 1 the Sixth and a portion of
the Nineteenth Corps returned via Washington to Gen.
Grant's army around Petersburg, while the Eighth
Corps remained in the Valley to the close of the war

The cavalry under Torbert remained in the Valley
until the last of February, 1865, when it marched over-
land to Petersburg, Va.

STRENGTH OF SHERIDAN'S ARMY IN THE VALLEY.

Sixth Corps.	13,322	Military District of	
Nineteenth Corps .	13,025	Harpers Ferry	4,815
Eighth Corps (army			
of West Virginia)	7,507	Total . .	45,487
Cavalry Corps.	6,818		

Losses.

Sixth Corps . .	4,899	Provisional Divi-	
Nineteenth Corps .	5,020	sion	732
Eighth Corps .	2,885		
Cavalry Corps . .	2,184	Total. . . .	16,721

Prisoners captured by Sheridan, 13,000.

The strength of Gen. Early's army was not over 30,000 at any one time, but being on the defensive could throw almost his entire strength against his antagonist.

As Gen. Sheridan advanced up the Valley he was compelled to leave a strong force along the route to protect his communications

During the greater portion of the campaign the Rangers were on special service in the military district of Harpers Ferry, under Gen. Stephenson. Their former brigade commander, Col Wells, 34th Massachusetts, was killed near Fisher's Hill, October 13, 1864

Many that followed the fortunes of Sheridan in the Valley distinguished themselves in after years Col. R B Hayes, commander 1st Brigade, 2d Division, Eighth Corps, rose to be President of the United States—1877-1880 He had a horse shot under him at Cedar Creek, and was himself wounded. Capt. R. A. Alger, of the Custer Brigade, became Governor of Michigan. Lewis A. Grant, of the Vermont Brigade, Sixth Corps, was Assistant Secretary of War under President Harrison's Administration. J. W. Keifer, a division commander of the Sixth Corps, served as a member of Congress and Speaker of the House of Representatives. Richard W. Blue, 6th West Virginia, W. A. Calderhead, 126th Ohio, of Kansas, E. F. Loud, 2d Massachusetts Cavalry, of California, L. J. Fenton, 91st Ohio, of Ohio, and B. B. Dovener, of West Virginia, all members of the 54th Congress, served under Sheridan in the valley. William McKinley, A A. G., First Division, Eighth Corps, has been a member of Congress and Governor of Ohio, and a host of others have been prominent in private life.

Many that followed the fortunes of the Lost Cause in the Valley have been heard from since the war. Gen. John B. Gordon, a corps commander, has been Governor of Georgia and United States Senator. Capt. John W.

Daniel, of Early's staff, is United States Senator from
Virginia. Governor O'Ferrell and ex-Governor Cameron served under Early. Quite a number of Confederates who followed the fortunes of Gen. Early in
the Valley have gone into the ministry since the war.

> ' While e'er the lamp holds out to burn
> The vilest sinner may return."

CHAPTER XII.

THE ADAMSTOWN FIGHT—GORESVILLE—FRENCH BILL, TRITAPOE,
AND BEST—DOWNEY'S MILL—HISTORIC SHENANDOAH VALLEY

October 14 the Rangers' patrol, from the Monocacy,
came in about 10 o'clock, and reported to Capt. Henry
Bartnete, provost marshal, that a force of about 300
rebel cavalry had crossed at Cheek's, or White's Ford,
and moved in the direction of Frederick.

A few minutes later several boatmen came rapidly up
the towpath and reported that Mosby's men had pillaged
and burned five canal boats, taken the stock, and moved
in the direction of Adamstown.

Capt. B. Spence, 1st Pennsylvania L. A., Battery G,
was in command of the post, and ordered Capt. Grubb,
of the Rangers, to move in the direction of Adamstown
and attack Mosby and force him back to the river,
while he, Capt Spence, would march with two companies of infantry down the river and await the return
of the raiders. As the latter drew nigh the river Capt.
Grubb was to charge their rear, while the infantry was
to attack in front.

Capt Grubb, with 81 men (all there was in camp at
the time), moved promptly to Adamstown and attacked
Mosby's force, under Maj. Chapman, and drove them
three miles to near the river. Much to our surprise,
Capt. Spence did not show up ; but we were in for it,
and made the best of a bad bargain.

The Rangers charged and poured several volleys into the raiders, who fell back to a strip of woods near the river, where they were re-enforced by two companies under Col. Mosby in person. This force now fell upon Capt. Grubb, who, in turn, fell back, endeavoring to save the command from as much damage as was possible. In this charge and countercharge Company A lost George Waters, killed; Robert W. Hough and Joseph Bagent, badly wounded. Sergt. J. N. Johnson and John Coates were made prisoners Company B lost Sergt. John W. Forsythe and Daniel Burnett, made prisoners. Mosby reports his loss as two missing.

These despatches, taken from the Official Records, vol. 43, refer to this raid .

"POINT OF ROCKS,
" *October 14, 1864*

"Brig. Gen. STEPHENSON.

"SIR . The rebels reported crossing at White's Ferry and moving towards Frederick, the boatman says, with a large force. I have sent the Loudoun Rangers to meet them.

"B. SPENCE,
"*Captain Commanding.*"

"HARPERS FERRY,
" *October 14, 1864.*

"Capt SPENCE,
"*Point of Rocks, Md.*

"Move out with all your infantry force to assistance of Capt. Grubb. If there are not more than 250 cavalry you ought to whip them easily.

"JOHN D. STEPHENSON,
" *Brigadier-General*"

"POINT OF ROCKS,
" *October 14, 1864—4 p. m*

"Gen STEPHENSON.

"I moved down the towpath to cut them off
"B. SPENCE,
"*Captain Commanding* "

November 27th Mosby's command was reported to be near Leesburg with a large force. Lieuts. Graham and Rhodes, with 39 men, crossed the Potomac late in the evening, and marched until about 2 o'clock a. m., resting until 8 o'clock a. m., November 28th We advanced towards Leesburg, which was found to be occupied by a detachment of Mosby's men. Lieut. Rhodes led a charge into town by the Winchester pike On our approach Mosby's men concealed themselves in the town. Two Confederate officers, mounted on fine horses, endeavored to escape by going out the pike east of town. Sergt Ed T. White, John S. Densmore, Joseph T. Ritchie and M. H. Best gave chase. Col Coleman, of the 5th Virginia Cavalry, was soon overtaken The other officer, riding a long, gaunt, roan horse, bid fair to escape. While crossing the railroad his horse fell, pinning the rider to the ground. As our boys rode up the officer cried out : " Gentlemen, won't you please get this horse off of my leg?" Densmore, Ritchie, White, and Best dismounted, and soon extricated Capt. Smith, A. A. G., of Gen. Early's staff. He was a son of ex-Governor "extra-Billy" Smith. Our brief acquaintance was exceptionally pleasant. As we took them back through Leesburg, some young ladies presented them with several friendly greenbacks to "cheer them on the way." Lieuts Graham and Rhodes marched their men for camp, going out the Point of Rocks road.

After we had passed the Limestone the men began to straggle—it was about 2 o'clock. The men had been in the saddle ever since early morning, and would fall out of line, endeavoring to get something to eat. The column was stretched out about one mile in length.

As the head of the column approached Paxton's Store, about 50 yards in their front, in a slight hollow on the Point of Rocks road, was formed in line of battle 250 of Mosby's men. They raised a yell and the firing began.

They recaptured our two prisoners and captured several of our boys beside. While this straggling in most cases would have proved disastrous, yet in this case it saved the company from heavy loss. Those who were near enough in front to go out the Taylorstown road were all captured, except Sam. Fry, who rode buckskin and escaped. Those that were further in the rear escaped, with perhaps one or two exceptions. Sergts. James H. Beatty, M. S. Gregg, and privates M. H. Best, Henry Cole and others went out through the Whipmore farm, and were closely pressed by Mosby's men, led by Capt. Mountjoy. This force had captured M. S. Gregg and were in close pursuit of the others. M. H. Best turned in his saddle, took deliberate aim, fired, and killed Mountjoy, the ball entering his brain. This ended the contest for the day. In the confusion that followed, M. S. Gregg escaped. Our loss in prisoners was Lieuts. Rhodes and Graham, John M. Davis, Webb Franklin, P. H. Heater, Peter Fry, John Lenhart , wounded, Graham, Lenhart, Peter Fry, and Jacob Cordell The latter was not captured. Mosby lost one killed, Capt. Mountjoy, and four wounded.

After Sheridan had made the Shenandoah Valley untenable for an army, many of the Confederates sought refuge in Loudoun, where forage and supplies were more plentiful The citizens in the German settlement had been greatly annoyed by raiders, principally Mosby's and White's men, under John Moberly and French Bill. This band generally had from two to twenty men, and would entirely disappear when any number of Federal troops was near.

Gen. Sheridan had instructed the commander at Harpers Ferry, Gen Stephenson, to break up this band if possible.

The matter was placed in the hands of the Rangers, and had to be done by small squads. Corporal S. E. Tritapoe, Joseph T. Ritchie, Joseph Fry, Company A, and Wilson Lathen, of Company B, were ordered to Virginia November 30 for that purpose It was learned that the band of mauraders was near Lovettsville By the aid of a light snow newly-made horse tracks were followed to the residence of Charles Johnson, a Union man, where one of the rebels was found ; he was full of fight and began shooting at his captors. Finally, Tritapoe and Ritchie clubbed the revolver out of his hand and made him their prisoner. This rebel was none other than French Bill, the notorious freebooter and murderer He was a deserter from both the 28th and the 61st New York Infantry, a professional bounty jumper, and was finally caught up with and fled and joined White's command, and became a boon companion of John Moberly, the guerilla. He and Moberly captured the surgeon of the 6th Pennsylvania Cavalry and brutally murdered him. French Bill was taken to Point of Rocks and turned over to Capt. H. Bartnete, provost marshal, who had him taken to Harpers Ferry and placed in the custody of Gen. Stephenson The following telegraphic correspondence, taken from Official Records, volume 43, part 2, pages 721–727, furnishes the tragic climax of the case, as well as the swiftness of cold-blooded military law ·

" Point of Rocks,
" <i>December 1, 1864.</i>

" Brig. Gen. Stephenson.

" * * * French Bill, of Moberly's freebooters, was yesterday taken by Keyes' men, I understand If so, he is an important capture, as he is a deserter from the 28th New York Infantry. * * * * Col. Root, of the 15th New York Cavalry, now at Pleasant Valley, will furnish you evidence against French Bill. Also a clerk in employ of Mr. Bush, who was sutler for 28th New York Infantry I will bring him to Harpers Ferry.

" D. Henry Bartnete,
" <i>Captain, etc.</i>"

"Harpers Ferry,
"*December 1, 1864,*

"Maj. Gen Sheridan.

"* * * I caught French Bill yesterday, a notorious murderer and bushwhacker, belonging to White's battalion, who was with the party that murdered the surgeon of the 6th Pennsylvania Cavalry. He is a deserter from the 61st New York Infantry.

"Respectfully,
"John D Stephenson,
"*Brigadier General Commanding.*"

"Headquarters Middle Military Division,
"*December 1, 1864—1.45 p. m.*

"Gen. Stephenson.

"*Commanding District of Harpers Ferry.*

"As soon as you can have fully ascertained that you have French Bill as your prisoner, take him out and hang him. This will be your authority.

"P. H. Sheridan,
"*Major General Commanding*"

"Harpers Ferry, *December 1, 1864*

"Maj. Gen. Sheridan.

"I have, undoubtedly, French Bill. He will be hanged at 2 p. m. to-morrow.

"John D Stephenson,
"*Brigadier General.*"

"Harpers Ferry, *December 2, 1864*

"Gen. Sheridan.

"French Bill has been hanged in accordance with orders.

"John D. Stephenson,
"*Brigadier General.*"

The affair is thus mentioned in headquarters correspondence·

> "BERLIN, *December 6, 1864.*
>
> "Brig. Gen. JOHN D. STEPHENSON.
>
> " * * * Corporal Tritapoe, who took French Bill, shot one of Mosby's men yesterday. He died this morning at Lovettsville. He is out again for more.·
>
> > "D. H. BARTNETE,
> >
> > " *Capt. and Asst. Provost Marshal.*"

The old worm-eaten story that "one rebel can whip five Yankees" was made ridiculous by the following incident Sunday, December 4, 1864.

Corporal Samuel E. Tritapoe and Mahlon H. Best obtained permission to visit their homes in Loudoun. This was the ground on which they obtained a pass to cross the river. Their true mission was a sparking expedition. It is presumed the reader is moderately well posted as to the nature of such expeditions, so that a fuller explanation is deemed unnecessary They crossed the river on the ferry boat about one o'clock, going through Lovettsville, where the young ladies waved a "God bless you" at them. About one mile beyond, two men on horseback were noticed approaching. Best jocularly remarked, "There come two Johnny rebs." As they met, all parties halted, with a pleasant "good afternoon." Corporal Tritapoe asked them where they were going, etc. The reply was, "we are hunting some cattle that disappeared while Sheridan was raiding and burning in the valley" Tritapoe began to get a little nervous, as he always did when going to see his best girl, and suggested to Best they had better ride on, but Best was not in a hurry. In fact, he was never known to be in a hurry. He was somewhat of an investigative turn of mind. It was just like him to inquire what kind of tails the cattle

Corp. SAMUEL E. TRITAPOE, Co. A.

MAHLON H. BEST, Co. A.

had and if they would have the same kind of tails when found, and if not, what kind of tails would they have, and a thousand of just such questions.

On this occasion, however, he developed a freak for trading. One of the rebels had a new United States horse blanket, and Best bantered him for a trade. The rebel accepted, both dismounted and unbuckled their saddles and traded blankets, even up. The other rebel held Best's saddle while he arranged the blanket. In the meantime, Tritapoe had ridden some little distance ahead. When everything was adjusted Best mounted and galloped off to catch up with Tritapoe; greatly to the latter's annoyance, the two rebels were following them. Tritapoe turned around and remarked to the two strangers if they continued to follow them they would be arrested and taken to Harpers Ferry. The rebels did not heed this threat, but continued to, follow. There was a sharp turn in the road and a barn standing on the extreme angle, entirely obstructing the view beyond. One of the rebels rode up by the side of Best with a cocked revolver, heretofore concealed under his coat, and suddenly pushed it into his face, with the prompt demand to surrender, or he would blow Best's head off. Both parties stopped still. Best at first played possum, saying, "Now, you wouldn't shoot me, would you?" and as quick as a cat grabbed the rebel's revolver with a grip of Hercules. Now the battle began in earnest, and there and then was brought on one of the liveliest and toughest rough-and-tumble general engagements of the war. Tritapoe and the other rebel were having a little private shooting match of their own. While Best and the first rebel were pulling and heaving at the revolver for dear life—bang, bang—it was nip and tuck to keep the bullets from hitting the wrong man, with the advantage decidedly favoring the rebel, because he held the butt end, while Best froze on to the end that shoots.

R—12

The rebel would say, "Let go of my revolver, you Yankee." Best made no reply, but pulled and tussled, finally they pulled each other off their horses, both falling in a heap in the road, but neither let loose of the revolver They wrenched, they pulled, they twisted. The rebel swore, but Best saved his wind and pulled.

Both parties rallied to their feet but continued the "tug of war" with renewed vigor, Best made a desperate pull—twist—jerk, and wrenched the revolver from the rebel's hand The latter jumped behind the barn, barely escaping a shot from his own weapon. Best now turned his guns on the forces shooting at Tritapoe, the third shot bringing down his man, who was mortally wounded ; he died the next day. Best and Tritapoe now turned their attention to the athlete that jumped behind the barn, but he had escaped. This ended the battle.

The Bavarian army at Blenhiem lost one-fourth of that army, the Duke of Wellington at Waterloo lost one-third of his army ; Gen. McDowell at first Bull Run lost one-tenth of his army , Gen. Lee at Gettysburg lost less than one-third of that army—but this engagement of Best and Tritapoe stands without a parallel. The enemy lost all their horses, arms and munitions of war, one-half of their army was slain, while the other half escaped bare-headed.

Best had his thumb terribly lacerated by the hammer of the rebel's revolver, and his paper collar smashed up generally.

Tritapoe had two bullet holes in his clothes ; neither was in a presentable condition to visit ladies, and they returned to camp that evening with their booty.

It was a shot from Tritapoe's revolver that did the killing

Capt. Keyes presented each of these heroes with the horse he captured as a partial recognition of his bravery.

About the first of December Lieut. Gover, with 40 men, left camp, crossing at Harpers Ferry, and going "Between the Hills." On entering Hillsboro we struck Company C, White's battalion, in command of Capt. Sam. E. Grubb. Lieut. Gover ordered a charge, driving them through the village. In the charge we captured four of their men, including the commanding officer, who was wounded One was killed, by the name of W. D. Gooding Several of our horses and one or two of the boys were hurt charging over a stone fence. We passed on through Wheatland, Waterford and Lovettsville, recrossing the river at Harpers Ferry.

The Capt Grubb above referred to is the same one we encountered at Neersville in September, 1863, previous.

December 24 Capt. Grubb, with 20 men (Companies A and B) dismounted, crossed on the ferry boat at 4 o'clock p. m to make a reconnaissance in Virginia

Geo. H. Harper, Joseph Fry, Dan Harper and Jack Virts, stopped for the night in the mountain. Sergt. Flemon B Anderson and Sergt. John P. Hickman, Company A, and Sergt. Geo. H. Hickman, Company B, stopped at Taylorstown. Briscoe Goodhart and M. H. Best went to visit home folks. Capt. Grubb and the balance of the squad continued on to Waterford, arriving at 7 o'clock p. m. There were 200 of White's Confederate cavalry camping one mile out of town.

Mrs Anderson, near Taylorstown, was giving a social party at her residence that evening. Her son, Sergt. Anderson, John and George Hickman were present with other young folks, enjoying themselves Sergt. Anderson was sitting beside a young lady, that rumor had was to be Mrs. Anderson some day.

About 9 o'clock the house was surrounded by 16 of White's and Mosby's men Ten of them entered the front door, with drawn revolvers. Sergt. Anderson attempted to escape by the back door, being near there As he arose his saber hook caught the chair back. In attempting to make his exit the chair caught on the door casing While extricating himself about ten shots were fired at him, three taking effect. With revolver in hand he was fighting like a tiger. As he gained the outside of the door he was shot through the head. In falling, his mother caught him in her arms, and he died in a few minutes.

Sergt Anderson was one of the best all-around soldiers in the command—of a quiet disposition, well-poised, and brave to recklessness. John and George Hickman were made prisoners, taken to Richmond and confined in Libby prison, and were exchanged in March

After they had surrendered one of the rebels wanted to shoot John Hickman for some alleged grievance ; the rebel snapped his revolver, but it missed fire. George Hickman appealed to their chivalrous spirit, saying, "We have surrendered like men and ask magnanimous treatment " One of the Bradens, of Mosby's command, who was related to the Andersons, interfered and put a stop to further bulldozing. Both of the Hickmans were excellent soldiers

In this affair the rebels had three wounded—Lieut. Chew, mortally, who died a few days afterwards. Eben Simpson was badly wounded. A sleigh was taken from Jule Fry, in which their wounded were conveyed to Mount Gilead that night. The Fry house was searched twice for George H and D J Harper, Joseph Fry, and Jack Virts, who had left a few minutes before.

Capt Grubb left Waterford on his return at 10 o'clock, arriving at Col. Giddings' at 12 o'clock midnight, where he remained for the night, and left the next morning, December 25th, at daylight. Before arriving at Taylorstown they learned of the sad and unfortunate affair at Mrs Anderson's. While stopping to view for the last time the remains of Sergt. Anderson, who had marched by his side only a few hours before, the tears rolled down Capt. Grubb's cheek.

Sergt. Flemon Benjamin Anderson was buried in Union Cemetery at Waterford, the next day, Monday, December 26th.

The balance of the squad returned to camp at 11 o'clock, with heavy hearts

As has been intimated in the course of this narrative, the Rangers were a moderately favored class with the fair sex All those that developed the slightest interest in matrimonial lines could with some slight effort enjoy reciprocity in that direction. In fact, each had his lady love The old adage, "True love does not run smooth," had, however, no exception in war times, or among the Rangers.

One of the fighting corporals of Company A had been very aggressive in his campaign with Cupid He had often contended against great odds, but his strategy, combined with his "staying qualities" when among the ladies, had never failed him. Nearly every mail brought encouragement to his heart, until during January, 1865, he received a letter that seemed to blast all hopes forever. His best girl had evidently been listening to some rebel. She wrote "In view of the uncertainty of the war, and in case we get married and the Confederates are successful, as recent developments seem to indicate, you would not be allowed to remain at home, and under such circumstances I deem it best for all concerned to sever our engagement "

This letter seemed at first to bring disappointment to all his plans; but, as has been stated, he possessed staying qualities in an immense degree, and resolved anew that the rebellion should be put down if he had to do it himself, as that seemed to stand in his road to future happiness.

Subsequent developments seemed to indicate that the corporal showed this letter to his confidential friends, and it soon got to be the news of the camp By some unknown way it fell into the hands of Sergt. James H. Beatty, who immediately pinned it on the front of the corporal's tent. The boys, supposing it was a bulletin from some recent battle, gathered around to read, About this time the corporal appeared, very angry, and then the entire camp yelled, "The corporal's girl has gone back on him." He drew his revolver and threatened to shoot the one who had put the letter on his tent ; but, of course, no one knew. It is but fair to state that the corporal dealt the Confederacy some heavy blows afterwards, and when peace reigned supreme he claimed his bride, and was married, and to-day enjoys the company of several younger "corporals," that have come to call him papa.

During the month of February, Sergt. James H Beatty, Henry Hough, Joe Ritchie, and George Davis obtained permission to go to Loudoun The river was high and roads were muddy, so the boys left their horses at camp and went on foot. Near Downey's still-house they struck the trail of four of Mosby's guerillas. The rebels had arrived at the still, dismounted, and gone into the house and filled their canteens with whisky. Sergt. Beatty and his men took position in the wagon shed. When the rebels came out to get on their horses, Sergt. Beatty's crew rushed out of the shed and opened fire on the enemy, capturing all four before they had time to draw their revolvers. From their foes our boys got eight revolvers and four excellent horses. One of the rebels was dubbed " Maj. Hibbs " He was one of Mosby's desperate characters, but not an officer, simply plain " Bill Hibbs." Another was Capt. James—a lieutenant—a judge—these titles were all assumed. Our boys mounted their horses and marched the four rebels ten paces in front, and in this order they were taken to camp.

A few weeks later Sergt. Beatty, Henry Hough and John Hickman went to Downey's. On entering the parlor, one of Mosby's men was sitting talking to Mrs Downey. Our boys took charge of him and asked him where his arms were, when he pointed to a chair in a corner of the room and said, "There they are " He never tried to get them, and did not seem to care whether the school kept, or not.

The first of March the command moved again to the Shenandoah Valley, camping near Keyes Switch, on the Shenandoah River. This section was first brought to public notice by George Washington, who established the first arsenal in the United States at Harpers Ferry (originally called Shenandoah Falls), soon after the Revolutionary War. There were kept here, before the war; about 75,000 muskets. The Chesapeake and Ohio Canal was for many years the only means of transportation to and from Washington.

The Harpers Ferry Arsenal, or Armory, was established in 1796, while George Washington was serving his second term as President of the United States.

There was purchased nearly 1,700 acres of ground at a cost of		$45,477
The improvements, consisting of buildings, water power, dams, etc , cost		1,787,430
Total		$1,832,907
Machinery and tools	$379,795	
Material and patterns . .	193,616	
Arms, etc., in store	285,146	
Total U. S property		$2,691,463

Near Charlestown there lived a trio of officers in the Revolutionary War whose histories were sadly similar—Horatio Gates, Charles Lee, and Adam Stephen—all three were with Washington at Braddock's defeat, all were wounded, all became general officers in the Continental army, all were court-martialed for misconduct on the field of battle and all found guilty.

Near Harpers Ferry, on the Potomac, there was invented by James Ramsey, in 1785, the first steamboat in the world, the machinery of which is now on exhibition in the National Museum at Washington.

The famous Shenandoah Valley, an Indian name, was originally called "Gerando" The Valley was first settled in about 1730, or 1732 This section drank long and deep of the bitter cup of war, in fact it was one continuous battle field for four long years. The traveler passing from Harpers Ferry, or Shepherdstown, to Staunton, a distance of 150 miles, is never out of sight of a battlefield. The second battle of the war was fought here at Harpers Ferry, April 18, 1861, six days after Fort Sumter was bombarded, and one day before the 6th Massachusetts was mobbed in the streets of Baltimore There were no less than 175 battles fought in the Valley from 1861 to 1865 Some localities can boast of as many as fourteen engagements, Winchester having had that number, and in ten of those battles artillery was used. Front Royal, Berryville, Charlestown, Harpers Ferry, and Shepherdstown lay claim to one dozen battles each.

Shenandoah Valley is often referred to in history as the "Valley of Humiliation" and the "Valley of Death," which is literally true in hundreds of cases. It was the valley of humiliation to Gen. Banks at Front Royal, to Gen. Milroy at Winchester, but doubly so to Gen. Early at Cedar Creek, at Fisher's Hill, and at Waynsboro. Why this valley should be selected as the stage where bloody and dramatic scenes of war were enacted was, probably,

because of its importance—a goodly land, that literally
flowed with milk and honey.

Previous to the war the farms produced forty to fifty
bushels of wheat to the acre, and will do the same to-
day with proper tillage.   It was also studded with flour
and grist mills and factories, and the choicest of fruits
in great abundance   Many Federal soldiers who served
here during the war were so favorably impressed with
this Garden of Eden of Virginia, that after the final act
at Appomattox, where the curtain rolled down and shut
out forever, let us hope, the bloody scene, settled here
and are to-day enjoying the fruits of their labors under
their own vine and fig tree.

As to the Confederacy, their choicest blood was poured
out here like water that they might retain possession of
this goodly land , and how well they succeeded, the hundreds and thousands of grassy mounds between Harpers
Ferry and Staunton will testify   It was also the natural
gateway between the North and the South , the Confederate army always passed through this valley going to, or
coming from, invading the North   Both after Antietam
and after Gettysburg their shattered armies sought refuge
and recuperation in the Shenandoah Valley.   The fighting in the Valley was exceedingly aggressive when cavalry and light artillery took a prominent part.   The ten
cavalry regiments that suffered the greatest loss of any
mounted troops during the war, namely, 1st Maine, 1st
Vermont, 1st New York Dragoons, 1st New Jersey, 5th
and 6th Michigan, 2d New York, 11th Pennsylvania,
and 8th Illinois, won their laurels in the valley with
Sheridan and Custer.

The future historian will find much here to repay for
research   We turn in vain to fiction to find where the
human mind in all its fertility of imagination has por-
trayed anything to compare with the battles of Cedar
Creek and Fisher's Hill.   Sheridan's ride stands without

a parallel. That which was actually fought out and demonstrated, the poet, artist and dramatist have loved to dwell on this scene, and have given to poetry and song some of its brighest gems.

Trowbridge says the Shenandoah Valley was supposed to have been a vast lake, or inland sea, that poured its majestic waters over the Blue Ridge, at Harpers Ferry, forming a cataract that dwarfed Niagara Falls into insignificance. As this is beyond the scope of this work, we shall not present evidence to substantiate the above claim, but leave the reader to investigate for himself

Charlestown is loaded down with war history. Gen Braddock's army bivouacked here after its defeat in western Pennsylvania "Braddock's Well," about half a mile west of town, is pointed out to the stranger, and had it been anything else but a well would have been carried off long ago as a war relic During the late war both Federals and Confederates slaked their thirst from this fountain Tradition says this well was dug at the suggestion of Gen Braddock's chief of staff, who was no other than Col Washington, afterwards Gen Washington and President George Washington. The town was named after the colonel's brother, Charles.

It was also the home of that talented Col D. H. Strother, " Porte Crayon," historian and artist, the progenitor of illustrated magazine articles which are now so popular , he was colonel of the 3d West Virginia Cavalry Regiment President Andrew Johnson appointed him Minister to Mexico in 1866 He died in 1886, rich in honors

It was here John Brown was brought from Harpers Ferry for trial, here convicted, and here executed for alleged treason, by being publicly hanged in an open field adjoining town, December 2, 1859

> " The case dismissed, the record closed,
>   The court adjourned, yet his soul
>   Went marching on."

The cause for which he died grew stronger and stronger with every pulsation of the great American heart, until it finally crushed out and expunged forever from the Constitution that foul blot of slavery

There lived a very interesting character about three miles south of town, on the Berryville pike, by the name of Jim Roper, who had quite a remarkable war history Perhaps the word war might be less emphatic ; in reality, he did not have any war history The story is a kind of a compromise between a tragedy and a romance

During the Mexican War every able-bodied man in this section was ordered to take up arms and march with Gen. Scott to Mexico. This man, Roper, who was of English descent, had immense possessions, and it grieved his heart to leave them He had a very dark complexion, and to escape going to war he swore he had African blood in his veins. The scheme worked like a charm; in fact, it worked a little too well, it not only kept him out of the war, but it kept him and his family out of society the rest of their days. Notwithstanding his great wealth his neighbors shunned him as they would a case of smallpox.

He had several fine-looking daughters, but they found no admirers in the neighborhood So far as company was concerned, they had just as well lived in the desert of Sahara. The old gentleman had several fine farms and offered one with each of his daughters to any man that would marry one, but the inducement did not prove sufficient for investors in live stock, until the close of the late war, one of E. V. White's Confederate guerrillas, by the name of Charles Cooper, married one of the daughters and got his farm. About the same time a German, by the name of William Shultz, who belonged to a New York regiment and "fit mit Sigel," married the other daughter and got his farm also. The old gentleman was shrewd enough to deed the farms to his daughters and their children

The last we heard of Cooper he had sold off all the good timber from his farm to raise a little cash, without work, and had squandered that and was about strapped · Shultz, coming from a race that had practiced great economy and industry, and had not forgotten these maxims in his new home, is now one of the successful farmers of the valley. The old gentleman died in 1870.

Berryville is another interesting old town, also known as Battletown. This place was the scene of a number of severe engagements Gen. Geary crossed swords here with Turner Ashby ; later Banks contended for supremacy with Jackson , next comes Milroy and Jackson, then Crook and Imboden. Wilson and Early fought a desperate battle here in the fall of 1864, nearly 8,000 cavalry being engaged. It was near here that Maj. Chapman surrendered Mosby's command, April 17, 1865, to Gen. Hancock's command. Less than a dozen miles from here his command murdered six members of the 5th Michigan cavalry about six months before After such a career for four years they were allowed to go in peace.

Verily, the fragrance of the apple blossoms at Appomattox cast their mellowing influence to Berryville. Sacred Writ furnishes the only parallel, " Though your sins be as scarlet, they shall be as white as snow ; though they be red like crimson, they shall be as wool."

Berryville was also the home of John Esten Cooke, the Confederate historian, also a member of Gen Lee's staff. He wrote the lives of Gens. Lee, Stonewall Jackson, Jeb Stuart, etc., and he wrote quite a number of works of fiction founded on the late war, of which the principal was "Surrey of Eagle's Nest," a work of considerable merit and of a wide circulation, particularly in the South.

About five miles southwest of Berryville in April, 1862, occurred one of the darkest, saddest and most inexcusable blunders of the entire war.

Gen Banks' army lay in the Valley near White Post. Blenker's division was at Paris, east of the Shenandoah River, near Snicker's Gap, and was ordered to Millwood, west of the river, and to cross at Berry's Ferry. The stream was swollen and very deep at this point, with swift current, with one old scow about 25 feet long to ferry them across. Gen. Bohlen's Brigade was crossing, the 54th and 58th New York and 74th Pennsylvania had crossed. Gen. Bohlen become impatient at this slow process, and in his rage, forgetting the old maxim of his own people (German), " slow but sure," proposed to take the short but very dangerous road to fame, and ordered his own regiment, the 75th Pennsylvania, to cross, putting 60 men of Companies A and B on board, when only 15 men had been taken over before ; and to economize space, as he claimed, he ordered every man to strap his knapsack on his back, packed the men on as closely as they could stand, and started for the other shore This excessive load caused the boat to begin to dip water from the start, and as the craft struck the current it sank, and 60 patriots went down to a watery grave. Every one of them was drowned, none of them ever rose to the surface, and not a body was ever recovered for respectable burial Had not Gen. Bohlen borne such an excellent reputation as a soldier, thoroughly infused with the spirit of patriotism, he would have been summarily dealt with , as it was, considerable loud talk was indulged in against him. The feeling was such that his usefulness in the brigade was ended, and at his own request he was transferred immediately and assigned to McDowell's division, where he commanded a brigade on the Rappahannock   Driven by remorse on account of the fatal error he committed on the Shenandoah, he resolved to redeem himself in the confidence of his countrymen; and, in leading a gallant charge at Freeman's Ford on the Rappahannock, four months later, August 22, 1862, he was riddled with rebel bullets and fell, a complete sacrifice, on the altar of his country.   Let it be said to his credit he died facing the enemy, and his example ought to have been followed by some of the other early commanders of the Army of the Potomac, whenever an error was made.

Five miles southwest of Millwood is White Post, a very interesting locality, now a small village, which takes its name from a large white post erected by Gen' George Washington   This ancient landmark stands in the center of the road, three feet thick at base and running up 15 feet in height to a point   It is inclosed by a chain railing for protection   It was erected to mark the center of that vast estate of Lord Fairfax, nearly six million acres, granted by the English Crown, embracing the territory between the Potomac and the Rappahannock Rivers, and east of the Alleghany Mountains.

General Washington surveyed this estate when he was less than twenty years old.   This was his introduction to public notice.

Lord Fairfax erected near here his residence, known as "Greenway Court."   It was one of the haunts of Washington   When the news of the surrender of Lord Cornwallis to Gen. Washington reached Lord Fairfax, who was very much attached to the British Crown, he said to his body servant, "Put me to bed, Joe ; it is time to die," and it was his death bed.   He never rallied, and died December 10, 1781.

CHAPTER XIII.

BACK TO HARPERS FERRY—THE RAID TO UPPERVILLE AND MID-
DLEBURG—FIGHT AT HAMILTON—CAPT KEYES RESIGNED ON
ACCOUNT OF WOUNDS—CAPT GRUBB COMMANDS THE BATTALION
—KEYES' SWITCH—JOHN MOBERLY—LEE SURRENDERS—THE
WAR IS OVER—RETROSPECTIVE—WAR FINANCES

: March 20 an expedition was started from Harpers
Ferry on an extended raid into Virginia, under sealed
orders—that is, the expedition was to go to Upperville,
Fauquier County, where the orders were to be opened,
etc   The raid was to be made with the following troops
Companies A and B, Loudoun Rangers, Capt. Grubb ;
five companies of the 12th Pennsylvania Cavalry, commanded by Col Reno , eight companies of 1st United
States Infantry, commanded by Lieut. Col. Bird, and
two pieces of light artillery   Col. Reno was in command of the expedition

We left Harpers Ferry about 1 o'clock, crossing the
Shenandoah River, going "Between the Hills"   At
Hillsboro we struck a squad of rebels, capturing five
who were sent back to Harpers Ferry   The expedition
moved on, and stopped for the night near Wood Grove.
Our pickets were fired into several times during the
night.

. The next morning, March 21, we marched to Purcellville, where the rebels were encountered in some
force , opened a bushwacking engagement on all sides,
but would not come near enough for our forces to strike
with effect. The column marched down the pike towards Hamilton, and the rebels marched along parallel
with our column, but kept about half a mile away.
They were also in our advance and rear about the same
distance. Whenever a hill or ravine would protect
them they would crawl near enough to the road to bush-

wack us, and we kept out a skirmish line on each side and rear, and an advance guard to prevent a surprise.

At Hamilton the rebels made a stand and endeavored to draw our forces into a trap. There is a crossroad running due south. On this road the enemy attacked our skirmish line, driving them in. The rebels slowly fell back into a piece of woods where their main force was concealed. As our cavalry advanced to a small rise of ground in the woods, the enemy suddenly charged from their ambush and drove our cavalry back in some confusion to near the pike, when our infantry opened on the rebels, driving them pell-mell in every direction.

In this engagement we lost nine killed and about twenty wounded and five prisoners. The rebels left three killed on the field and an artillery officer, named Chew, dangerously wounded. Their wounded that could be moved were taken with them. It was learned afterwards they had two deaths among their wounded.

The rebel forces engaged were Mosby's, White's, and Early's commands. The rebel officer left belonged to Bradley T. Johnson's brigade of Early's corps.

Our forces camped for the night in Hamilton. We buried our dead that evening in the graveyard adjoining town. It rained hard during evening and the early part of the night. Our pickets were fired into during the night, as usual.

The next morning, March 22, our column moved back to Purcellville, with the same bushwhacking crowd on our flanks and rear. We continued on the pike to Snickersville, where we turned south, stopping for the night near Bloomfield. Here the bushwhackers made some demonstration, particularly in noise.

March 23 we moved into Upperville, where the rebels were found in some force, but they withdrew on our arrival. We picked up two stragglers in the streets. The direction was changed here to east. The bushwhackers

WHITE POST.—Erected by George Washington and Lord Fairfax, to mark the center of that vast estate granted to Lord Fairfax by the British Crown; also to direct the traveler to "Greenway Court."

were more annoying than ever. They would attack our force with terrific yelling and fire a few shots, but would not venture near enough to get hurt While our column was crossing Goose Creek bridge Mosby made an unsuccessful effort to capture our wagon train, or run it off into the creek. The enemy was concealed in a hollow near the bridge, and after our troops had crossed they were to rush upon the train and capture or destroy it. There were several squads of the enemy stationed on the hills in full view of the bridge, and at the proper time they were to signal with looking glasses for their main force to charge.

The Rangers crossed about ten minutes in advance of the other troops and discovered the looking-glass signals, and the force concealed in the hollow, and reported the facts to Col. Reno, who placed the infantry and the two pieces of artillery near the eastern end of the bridge until the train was over At a certain time the enemy began their looking-glass signals, when their forces poured from their place of concealment like a swarm of bees, charging towards the bridge, yelling like coyotes, but when they saw the infantry and artillery waiting to receive them, their hearts failed them, and they gave up the job Several shots were fired, but the range was too long for any damage.

The column moved on towards Middleburg, where we captured three of Mosby's men.

The column now turned north, striking Little River pike, where we met the 8th Ill Cavalry, Col Gamble, with two pieces of artillery, that came up from Washington

We crossed Goose Creek again about 15 miles further down, but Mosby did not try to run us off the bridge at this crossing, probably because the bridge had been destroyed.

The next day, March 23, we arrived at Hamilton,

R—13

where we captured two rebels. We stopped for the night at good, loyal, old Waterford.

March 24 we arrived at the Ferry.

Col. Reno gained some notoriety in connection with the Gen. Custer massacre in 1875, on the plains of Montana.

The close of every twenty-four hours demonstrated most fully and beyond question that the days of the Confederacy were numbered and very few, yet the Confederate bands that inhabited Loudoun grew more desperate in their attitude towards the citizens of that county. It was almost impossible for the citizens to keep horses, as bands of guerrillas would take them. In many cases it was known that this stock was appropriated for their own use, although the Confederate government was directly responsible. As early as April, 1862, that alleged government passed an Act authorizing the recruiting of guerrilla bands, who were to receive compensation for their service from horses and other property taken from Union citizens. This was nothing more nor less than an attempt to legalize horse-stealing. A government that would attempt such legislation was badly in need of a conscience Mosby's band was organized and fostered under the provisions of the above act. While White's command was originally recruited as regular Confederate cavalry, he afterwards obtained his largest number of recruits under the Act referred to.

Perhaps the most desperate band of this military banditti was John Moberly's, who belonged to White's command, although he committed the most of his atrocious deeds on his own hook. He had become so desperate and such a terror to the citizens that Gen. Stephenson, the commander at Harpers Ferry, found it absolutely necessary to offer a reward for his body. A detail of twelve of the Rangers was ordered to the Loudoun Valley to capture or kill Moberly and his band The band had, at most, about twelve men, although generally only three or four.

This squad of the Rangers learned where Moberly was expected to be, and endeavored to catch him at that place. They concealed themselves and waited, and it was not long before he approached, coming down the road, with drawn saber, chasing a negro boy who was driving a cart. The boy was badly frightened, which Moberly seemed to enjoy. As he approached, our boys rose to their feet and demanded a surrender. Moberly lay down in his saddle, put spurs to his swift-footed horse, and, making a sharp turn in the road, darted out of sight. Every one of our boys fired at him at close range, but did not strike him. We were on foot and could not follow, but returned to camp without the coveted game.

A few days after, Capt. Keyes resigned, on account of a broken leg, and Lieut Gover acted as captain of Company A, while Capt Grubb, of Company B, commanded the battalion to the close of the war.

April 1 news arrived that Petersburg had fallen. Five days later the same wires brought news of the evacuation of Richmond. This news was enjoyed by all. The command was camped on the Shenandoah River, while twenty men of Company A were detailed on special duty at the provost marshal's office in Harpers Ferry

April 5 parts of Companies A and B were absent on a raid, leaving the camp in charge of Lieut. Gover, with fragments of both companies The Confederate army had been defeated at every recent engagement, and we were daily expecting to hear of its collapse. In such a state of expectancy military discipline was at a low ebb.

April 6 the command, or rather what few were at the camp, were taking their ease when a body of about 250 men in blue uniform approached from the northwest, or the Charlestown pike; little attention was given, as it was supposed this was a body of Custer's cavalry, that was known to be in the Valley. The column came up to less than 50 yards, when they dashed into our camp, capturing the majority of the few that were there This force proved to be Mosby's command, who thus approached our camp under the guise of Federal troops We had about 20 broken-down horses in camp, and most of them were taken. As they undertook to recross the Shenandoah River our pickets, that were stationed there in charge of George V Kern, opened fire on them, wounding several. One picket, Frank Kidwell, of Company B, was dangerously wounded, and left on the field for dead. Richmond having fallen into Federal hands, these prisoners were kept in custody by Mosby about one week and paroled

Eleven days after this event this same command (Mosby's) surrendered to the troops of our corps (Eighth) near Berryville

April 11 the news flashed over the wires that Gen. Lee's army had surrendered This was no great surprise, as we were daily expecting such news

April 15, while this country, from the Atlantic to the Pacific, was happy in the thought that the war was about over, the people were suddenly cast down in great sorrow over the unfortunate and untimely death of the immortal Lincoln.

Vice-President Andrew Johnson, of Tennessee, was sworn in as President of the United States.

During the spring of 1865 the guerilla, John Moberly, and his gang had become such a terror to that section of Virginia that to stand him longer was impossible. They murdered citizens and took their property and converted it to their own use without cause or provocation. They also gathered up negroes and took them to parties whom he asked to take them into the Union lines and enlist them in the Union army and get the bounty and divide with him Gen. Stephenson, commanding at Harpers Ferry, fully determined to break up this outrageous business

April 1 some of the citizens of that section proposed to Gen. Stephenson that if the Government would compensate them liberally, and also furnish them with means to live away from home, they would pilot a squad of soldiers to Moberly's retreat, where he and his gang could be either killed or captured.

Gen. Stephenson referred the matter to Gen. Hancock, who was in command of the department. Gen. Hancock opposed offering a reward openly, but stated in a communication that the parties would be liberally rewarded in proportion to their services, and approved the measure.

Monday, April 3, Gen. Stephenson ordered the commander of the Rangers to send to his headquarters a squad of three men. The men selected were Sergt Charles B. Stewart, Company B, Joseph Waters and M. H. Best, Company A, and they with three citizens proceeded to Virginia on foot

The general informed Sergt Stewart that he was to proceed, with a guide, to the mountains, where Moberly would probably be found, and capture, or kill him, and bring him to the Ferry. Stewart proceeded to the Short Hill, where he learned from reliable citizens that Moberly would be at a certain rendezvous some time the next day. Stewart's party rested for the night in a barn, and the next day proceeded to the appointed place, concealed themselves in a hay loft, and waited developments. In the afternoon of April 5, Moberly, accompanied by one man, approached directly towards where Stewart's men were concealed. Moberly rode into the barnyard, and under a shed, Stewart's men now revealed themselves, with drawn revolvers, when Moberly was heard to proclaim, "Oh, Lord, I am gone "

All fired, and Moberly fell from his horse, dead, thus ending his career. The other rebel, who was some distance behind him, turned his horse and escaped

On Moberly's tombstone, erected by his lady friends, is found this epitaph .

> " He has fought his last battle,
> He sleeps his last sleep,
> No sound on earth can awake him to glory again "

The next day the dead rebel's boon companions visited the place where their leader was killed, and burned the barn and contents of hay, grain, etc., and Uncle Sam paid the owner, Luther H. Potterfield, $2,500

The parties received $1,000, besides their expenses while living at Harpers Ferry, but the Rangers got no part of it.

The following correspondence, on file in the War Department, refers to the case :

"HARPERS FERRY, *April 5, 1865.*

"E M STANTON

"I sent out, on Monday, a small party to wipe out the notorious guerilla, Moberly, and his band. They returned to-day with the body of Moberly, and in the fight mortally wounded his right-hand man, Riley.

"Respectfully,

"J. D STEPHENSON,
"*Brig.-Gen Commanding* "

"WAR DEPARTMENT,
"*Washington, April 5, 1865*

"Brig.-Gen. STEPHENSON,

Harpers Ferry.

"Accept the thanks of the Department for your diligence, skill, and success in the achievement mentioned in your telegram of this date.

"EDWIN M. STANTON,
"*Secretary of War.*"

About the 20th of April Capt. E W Andrews (5th New York Heavy Artillery), provost marshal at Harpers Ferry, received a dispatch from Washington stating that parties supposed to be implicated in the assassination of the late President Lincoln were near Hagerstown, Md , and to proceed immediately to that point and arrest all parties under such charge. Capt. Andrews, with an escort of 20 of the Rangers, under Sergt. Joseph T. Divine, started from Harpers Ferry about 3 o'clock p. m., and arrived at Hagerstown about 7 o'clock p. m. He went four miles into the country and arrested the suspected parties and lodged them in the Hagerstown jail

We remained all night at Hagerstown During the early part of the night, John McDevitt imbibed a little freely of "commissary," and climbed up on some boxes in front of the Washington House, and went to sleep. While in this condition he rolled off and fell to the sidewalk, a distance of about twelve feet The fall nearly killed him, but he recovered sufficiently to be taken to Harpers Ferry the next day, where he was laid up for repairs for several days.

April 26 Gen Joseph E. Johnston surrendered to Gen. Sherman

May 20 Gen. E Kirby Smith surrendered This was the last of the organized forces of the Confederacy

The Federal troops began to be mustered out of service.

May 30 the Independent Loudoun (Va) Rangers were mustered out at Bolivar, West Va., lacking twenty days of serving three years.

They were glad the war was over; glad that the principles for which they fought had triumphed ; glad that the question was settled forever—that this is a Nation and not a confederation of States ; glad that the arbitrament of arms, the court of last resort, had decreed that slavery should no longer degrade American labor ; glad

they were part and parcel of a Nation that shall stand
without a parallel on the face of the earth

Retrospective.

If you ask the veteran of either side when the war
began he will tell you 1861   That is correct, so far as
open hostilities is concerned ; but in reality the war
began with the first importation of African slaves in
1619, over eighteen months before the Puritans landed
on Plymouth Rock.

It was not the difference in people that fostered
slavery in America , neither was it the climate.   It was
the chosen methods rather than either

The English Cavalier and the Puritan descended
from the same British stock   The first settlers at Jamestown gradually led in population up to 1790.   In that
year the South had a population equal to the Middle
States and the New England States combined   The
Great West was yet unborn

While slavery existed in a very few Northern States,
it was repulsive to the great mass, and was soon abol-
ished, while at the South it flourished and was popular.
At this period the North and the South began rapidly to
diverge.

From 1790 to 1830 the North gained a million more
in population than the South.   Thirty years later (1860)
it had gained six millions more.   The foreigner, seeking
a home in America, could not be induced to settle in
the South, because he could not compete with slave
labor.   Of the four millions that came to our shores
during this period less than one per cent settled in the
South.   As to natural resources, the South possessed
advantages superior to the North.   The immense de-
posits of coal, iron, copper, and salt in Virginia, Tennessee, Kentucky, Alabama, and North Carolina are not

surpassed in the North, while in climate, soil, and timber the South has been highly favored

With these natural advantages, the South ought to have been filled with manufactories, and it would have been had it not been for slavery.

While the North was forging ahead, adding wealth and population, building manufactories as monuments to its industry and prosperity, the South was building monuments of human slavery, which finally crumbled, tottered, and fell, and crushed the builders

War Finances

When President Lincoln came into office, the 4th day of March, 1861, he found the public treasury empty, the National debt over $76,000,000, and the Government borrowing money at 12 per cent   In less than sixty days public confidence had been sufficiently restored to enable the Administration to negotiate a loan of over $5,000,000 at 6 per cent.   After the commencement of the war public credit became temporarily impaired, which necessitated an additional loan of $7,000,-000, at 10 per cent.   The tariff was low, producing an income of but about $30,000,000 annually   The President convened Congress July 4, 1861.   That body passed an act July 17, 1861, for the issue of nearly $300,000,000 Treasury notes   "The baby was born, and its name was Greenback."   The National Banking Law was enacted by this Congress.   The Government was now provided with ample funds to carry on the war, although the terrible strain on the country depreciated the currency to a considerable extent   The private soldier's pay was $13 per month, with rations and clothing, and it cost the Government over $1,000 per year to maintain each soldier in the field.

At the beginning of 1862 there was a premium of 2

per cent. on gold ; at the end of that year it was 33 per
per cent. ; December, 1863, it was $1.50 ; June, 1864, it
was $2, making the greenback dollar worth just 50
cents July 11, 1864   When the rebel army of Gen.
Early was encamped at Silver Springs, a suburb of
Washington, preparing to attack the Capital, gold
touched its high-water mark, $2.85.

By the census of 1860 the real and personal property
of the United States was over sixteen thousand million
dollars.   The actual cost of the war, not including pen-
sions, was about half of that amount, or, in other words,
the cost of the war placed a mortgage of 50 cents on
every $1 in the United States

A protective tariff was enacted.   Congress also passed
a direct, or income tax, whereby the enormous expense
of carrying on the war was to be obtained by an equita-
ble distribution of the burdens among the masses.   All
luxuries were heavily taxed, while the necessaries of life
were moderately taxed.

Confederate Finances.

The Confederate finances were erratic and adventurous
from the beginning   There appears to be no record, or
report to be found among the rebel archives giving the
amount of money issued by that government, yet there
is evidence that the amount far exceeded the combined
value of the real and the personal property in the
seceded States.   It was issued by the million in Montgomery and Richmond, and in addition in the Southern
States, some county courts were empowered to issue
such amounts as "were necessary" to meet the "various
wants" of the authorities in support of the Confederacy,
etc.   In fact, the only limit to the volume of Confederate money was in the capacity of the presses to print it.

On one occasion the Secretary of the Confederate Treasury sent to their congress a report in which was stated the

outstanding debt. The next day the report was withdrawn on account of a trifling error—the error was $400,000,000. What the sum total must have been would baffle the imagination of a Wall street magnate.

This money rapidly depreciated until there was but little, if any, value to it, aside from what it was worth for old paper After the battle of Chancellorsville, when Confederate hopes seemed brightest, their money went begging in Richmond at $1 for ten cents in greenbacks. At the close of 1864 it took $500 in Confederate money to buy $1 in greenbacks in Richmond.

The following story will illustrate the value the public placed on that money :

A countryman was riding a common scrub through their camp, when an officer hailed him, offering him $50,000 for the animal. The rider gruffly replied, " No, sir ; I just paid $1,000 to have him curried this morning."

The South largely abandoned raising cotton and farming during the war, and, with but few factories, there was comparatively little revenue to be derived from any source.

The government was not democratic in form, but rather had monarchical tendencies. The edict of their President was almost supreme. They never had a Supreme Court, or a Judiciary, as a check on the Executive, or Legislative branches. There was no question raised as to constitutionality. Might was right with them It was common to argue and settle questions at the point of the bayonet ; in short, military law was the law of their land President Davis vetoed thirty-eight bills during the four years of the Confederacy's existence, but one, an unimportant measure, was passed over his veto. The bill provided for carrying newspapers to the soldiers without the payment of postage. During the same period President Lincoln vetoed but three bills.

CHAPTER XIV

A DARK CHAPTER — PRISON EXPERIENCES — LIBBY — CASTLE
THUNDER—PEMBERTON—BELLE ISLE—ANDERSONVILLE

" Whether in the prison pen,
Or in the battle's van,
The noblest place for man to die
Is where he dies for man "

This work would be incomplete without giving at
least a brief account of those of the Rangers who suffered, as well as those that died, in Southern prisons.

We have no apology to offer for the recital of the revolting details of this chapter.   It is a matter of history,
and history has no value unless it is correct.

An eminent artist presented for inspection a picture
of Rome he had just finished, and some of the critics
pronounced it a work of fine art, but concluded by saying it was rather dark, whereat the gifted artist grew
eloquent, with the remark that a " true picture of Rome
must be dark, as it was a dark subject."   So with the
picture of Southern prisons.

The Confederate prisons form the darkest chapter in
the blood-stained annals of this nation, and conclusively
prove that a people of a section guilty of such barbari-
ties to those within their power were totally unworthy
of, and unfit for, separate nationality.

All those that were so unfortunate as to fall into the
hands of the enemy, as prisoners, received bad enough
treatment ; some were treated like brutes, while others
fared worse than brutes.

As it will be impossible to give the individual experience of all, the writer will give the actual experience
of those who were made prisoners at Charlestown.   It
is perfectly reasonable to presume that others received

equally as bad, while many received much worse treatment.

The first of the Rangers taken prisoners and not paroled were J. H. Corbin and Joseph Waters, at Waterford, August 27, 1862 Corbin escaped at Culpeper Court House, while Waters was taken to Richmond and confined in Libby prison, where he remained about three weeks and was exchanged

Those taken prisoners at Leesburg, September 2, 1862, were Jacob Cordell, Jacob Long, George W. Baker, Charles Baker, Peter Miles, Armistead Everhart, George Welch and William Shoemaker; and of these, Everhart and Long were badly wounded and paroled.

George W. Baker and Jacob Cordell gave their names as belonging to Cole's Cavalry and were exchanged at once.

Charles Baker, Peter Miles, William Shoemaker and George Welsh, who gave their names as belonging to the Rangers, were confined in Castle Thunder, to remain during the war.

Baker, Miles and Shoemaker died there, actually starved to death; Welch remained until Richmond, in 1865, was evacuated, when he was released by the Union troops

Charles F. Anderson, Joseph T. Cantwell, John W. Forsythe and W H Angelow, having been paroled at Waterford, August 27, except Anderson, all were arrested at Point of Rocks, or Leesburg, and taken to Richmond. They gave their names as belonging to Cole's Cavalry and were soon exchanged.

Charles A. Webster, who left the company in November, 1862, soon thereafter was reported to be in the hands of the enemy. It was reported he went there as a spy; another report states he went there and gave himself up and offered to furnish information concerning the Union army, etc Both of the above reports

came through rebel sources.   A letter from a prominent historian, now in the possession of the writer,
states that Webster was captured in Loudoun County,
Va., in December, 1862

It has also been claimed that he went there with the intention of shooting Col. White and escaping, as nothing
was too risky for him ; the reward for this he knew would
be a promotion.   The fact that Col. White had had
Webster bucked and gagged, against the protest of
every one of his officers, seemed to furnish a reason for
this report.

Webster was taken to Richmond and confined in
Castle Thunder.   It was not long before he had his entire
floor organized into a plan of escape.   As usual, there
was a Judas in the crowd, and the plan was revealed to
the rebel authorities.   For this offense Webster was handcuffed and secured by a chain to a post in the center of
the room.   One afternoon in January, 1863, while the
prisoners were permitted to go to the lower floor for
water, etc, William Bensinger, of the 22d Ohio, a fellow
prisoner, who was confined there for being one of the
parties (Andrew's raiders) who captured a locomotive
at Big Shanty, Ga., and ran it to Chattanooga, made a
bone key and unlocked Webster's handcuffs and hurried
him down stairs with the other prisoners, and concealed
him in the basement, by covering him with tobacco
stems, where he was to remain until evening, when he
was to escape   When the other prisoners returned to
their room Webster was missed by the Confederates and
a search instituted, he was found and again handcuffed.
A blacksmith was brought in and riveted irons on his
ankles that would not allow him to step over twelve inches   In about ten days he was removed to the third
floor, his irons remaining on him.   He managed in some
way to slip his handcuffs and break the irons from his
legs, and after dark jumped from the third-story window

and fell in a pile of rubbish, breaking both legs. He dragged himself into a lumber yard near and hid The next day he was missed from prison, and late in the day he was found concealed in a pile of lumber, and was again shackled and placed in a dungeon Early in March, 1863, he was taken out of prison for trial, being charged with the murder of Capt. Simpson (see page 31), of the 8th Virginia Infantry, and also for violating his parole.

Gen. R. L. Wright, Isaac Van Deventer, John Ross, and H. S. Williams, Sr., of Loudoun, were summoned as witnesses against him.　It will be noticed that Webster was not allowed any witnesses, or even a defense of any kind.

H. S. Williams, of Taylorstown, testified that Webster came to his mill, bearing arms, in charge of a squad of the Rangers, after flour.　The arms he carried were those Col. White permitted him to retain in the terms of the capitulation at Waterford.　As a matter of course, he was convicted, and by the same kind of a trial he might have been convicted of crucifying the Saviour.

April 10, 1863, he was executed, by hanging, at Camp Lee (old Fair Ground), Richmond.　About two thousand prisoners from Castle Thunder and Libby were marched out to witness the hanging.　Webster was taken to the place of execution in a closed carriage, accompanied by the Rev. Mr. Brown and detectives New and Capehart of the Confederate service

On account of his broken legs he was unable to stand, and was carried, seated in a chair, to the scaffold, where he was given an opportunity to say a few words, which he delivered in his usual clear, ringing voice, while sitting erect in the chair.　He denounced the Confederacy in unmeasured terms, also Jeff. Davis, Col. Alexander, keeper of Castle Thunder, and Capt. Capehart, the Confederate detective.　He declared his innocence of the charges, and finally declared his undying allegiance to the United States and the Stars and Stripes. At his own request, he gave the signal by tossing his hat amongst his fellow-prisoners. The drop fell and Webster was no more.

The story, given currency by the rebels, that he confessed the charges and that five women called at the prison, each claiming him as her husband, was a wilful and malicious falsehood

Now as to his True Name

From the beginning to the end he was known to the Rangers as Webster, but that was not his name. His true name was Charles Brown He was born in New Hampshire and moved with his parents to Weld, Maine, where he grew to manhood. On the discovery of gold in California, his father went to the Golden Gate to dig out his anticipated fortune, leaving Charles to care for himself. On the breaking out of the war, Charles enlisted in the United States army, whether as Brown or Webster we are unable to state He, however, took the name of Webster from his mother, who was distantly related to Daniel Webster, the great Senator and orator from Massachusetts.

Soon after the battle of Antietam, while the 10th Maine Infantry lay near Brunswick, some members of that regiment, who knew Brown in Maine, recognized him with the Rangers and addressed Him as Charles Brown. It was said by his acquaintances in Maine that he took the name of Webster because his father was a malignant Copperhead (anti-war Democrat). The remains of Webster (Brown) are buried in the National Cemetery at Richmond, Va.

Webster married Miss Alice Downey, of Loudoun, in the fall of 1862. She died some time thereafter, his widow.

CHARLES A. WEBSTER (Brown), Drill Master.

Corp. GEORGE H. HARPER, Co. A.

June 17, 1863, Joseph T. Ritchie, M. S. Gregg, Chas. Pekam and John W Virts were taken prisoners at Point of Rocks They were confined in Pemberton and on Belle Isle ; their sufferings were severe. Charles Pekam died there, the others were exchanged in August.

At Neersville, September 30, F. P. Rinker and James Stoneburner were made prisoners. They were confined on Belle Isle all the fall and winter of 1863-4. In March they were sent to Andersonville, where they both died, actually starved to death

At Charlestown October 18, 1863, 18 of the Rangers were taken prisoner and perhaps suffered the greatest of any, as 14 out of the 18 literally starved to death. We shall briefly give their experience.

From Charlestown they were marched up the Valley to Staunton, where they were placed on cars and taken to Richmond, arriving one week from the date of capture. On being made prisoners the first thing demanded was their arms. The next, their money and other valuables, although quite a number managed to save their money, watches, etc , by concealing them in the seams of their clothing and in their stockings. Their treatment was very bad from the beginning. The rations furnished en route to Richmond were about half enough in quantity and of a very poor quality.

They arrived in Richmond Monday evening, November 1, and were placed in Pemberton prison, a three-story brick building (tobacco warehouse) on Cary Street, opposite Castle Thunder. The prison was in command of Maj. Turner, assisted by Erastus W. Ross. It was difficult to tell which of these two specimens of humanity was the more brutal, with the chances favoring Ross. He was very small in body, and still smaller in soul, if he had any.

On Tuesday the prisoners were all put on the upper floors, one being brought down at a time. The name, company, and regiment of each man was taken, and he was caused to disrobe himself, and while in this nude condition his clothes were turned, the seams and pockets all examined and thoroughly searched, his watch, money, pocket-knife, and all other valuables taken and placed on a table, with the guileless promise that these articles would be returned when the prisoner was exchanged. This promise, like all other promises of the Confederacy, was never fulfilled.

From the 9th Maryland and the Rangers and 1st New York Cavalry, about 375 men, the rebels obtained over $1,200 in greenbacks, and about sixty watches. This was an average of about $3 from each prisoner, and a watch from every sixth man. The Confederates captured during the war about 180,000 Union prisoners ; and, taking the above as a basis, the Confederates obtained no less than half a million dollars in greenbacks and thirty thousand watches and thousands of pocket-knives, etc , from their prisoners This estimate does not include what was taken from the prisoners on the field of battle and en route to prison, which was at least half of their possessions, and generally all of them.

What became of this property ? The Confederate archives are silent on this point This Ross, above mentioned, took charge of this property in Richmond. The few years he lived after the war were years of plenty He lost his life by the burning of the Spotswood Hotel in Richmond in 1869, his body being entirely consumed by the flames.

All prisoners that were so unfortunate as to pass under his blighting touch were unanimous in the belief that eventually he would be consumed by everlasting fire, but were loth to believe he was to receive a foretaste so soon

Their stay in Pemberton was brief, though long enough, just one week, and they were taken to Belle

Isle, in the James River, opposite Richmond.   So far as nature is concerned, it is a beautiful landscape.   It contains about thirty acres   The ground rising rapidly at the upper end, forming a ridge, or small mountain, while on the lower end it is a level, sandy plain, where the prisoners were confined in a square enclosure containing about two acres, surrounded by an embankment, or parapet, 5 feet high.   There was a ditch on the outside, 4 feet wide, and on the outside of this ditch the guards walked to and fro.   On the inside of the parapet was a ditch 4 feet deep and 6 feet wide, which was known as the "dead line," and woe be to him who ventured near

The stockade, or prison pen, contained a few old tents sufficient to accommodate 3,000, although there were double that number crowded into them   Eleven thousand was the greatest number of prisoners on this two acres at any one time, by which it will be readily seen several thousand were without shelter to protect them from the cold winter blasts.   Generally, when captured, the prisoners were deprived of their blankets and overcoats, and in consequence many were actually frozen to death   During the month of December the United States was permitted to send a few blankets and some clothing to the prisoners, who were in great need. These supplies were sent in charge of a young man, who distributed them to the prisoners   This young man was D. L. Moody, now the great evangelist.

The ration was a piece of corn bread, made from unsalted and unsifted meal, and about two inches square, which was generally furnished twice but often once a day, and sometimes once in two or three days, with occasionally a very small morsel of meat, or half a pint of bean soup.   On several occasions it was weeks that they did not receive anything but corn bread.   On this ration the prisoners became reduced rapidly in flesh. Without meat or salt, scrofula set in, and before spring no less than 5,000 actually perished, frozen and starved to death.

Capt. Bosson a French gentleman, was commandant of the Island, assisted by Lieut. Haight. The latter had the management of the prisoners and proved to be more of a tyrant then Ross, whom they were glad to leave over in Richmond

The numerous friends of the prisoners in the North forwarded hundreds, yes thousands, of boxes of provisions and clothing to Richmond, but not more than one in twenty-five was ever delivered, the rebels appropriating their contents to their own use Several boxes were shipped from Point of Rocks to the Rangers in prison. In some instances two and three boxes were addressed to the same person. John Heater forwarded three boxes to his son, Buck, but not one was ever delivered Lieut. Maginnis, of the 18th Connecticut, afterwards killed in battle, recognized a suit of citizen's clothes, sent him from the North, on the back of one of the prison officials ; he pointed out his own name worked on the watch pocket by his mother. According to the report of Col. Ould, Confederate Commissioner of Exchange, he received nearly four thousand of such boxes at Richmond alone. He received three hundred boxes one week in January, 1864, and delivered six of them to the owners Early in January, 1864, a large box was sent over from Richmond to Belle Isle. Lieut. Haight informed the prisoners it was from " God's Country," he ordered a squad to come out and open and carry in the contents. The box was from the United States Christian Commission, which society had forwarded quite a number of boxes filled with delicacies to the famishing prisoners, which were greatly enjoyed, and in this case they knew it contained something extra good ; such as sugar-cured hams, dried beef, cheese, etc., just what the starving prisoners were wishing All eyes were turned with bright anticipations upon the opening of this box, but instead of the hams, etc , rolling out, it contained nearly one thousand copies of the New Testament. It would be impossible to describe the sad disappointment of the prisoners, a cold-wave flag was apparently visible on every countenance.

It was the physical man that was perishing for bread on Belle Isle, and not the spiritual. However, the prisoners accepted their Testaments, with the wish that each had been a piece of meat as large. There was no danger of the rebels appropriating the contents of this box to their own use.

As winter rolled on the prisoners became weaker and weaker, until death by starvation and exposure relieved thousands from suffering It was a common occurrence to see poor fellows lie down and die in a few minutes.

The following experience fairly represents what was constantly occurring : Three of the Rangers, P A Davis, Ruben Stypes, and the writer, slept together on the sand. We were more fortunate, perhaps, than many of the other prisoners, as we had two blankets for the three—one under and one over us. Stypes was rather delicate, and it was with some difficulty that he could eat what little corn bread he received He slept in the middle, being better protected from the cold. He had been complaining for several days, and that evening, January 20, he cut the crust from his bread, gathered up a few splinters, toasted it, made a cup of coffee and enjoyed it. We all lay down at dark and endeavored to sleep. About 12 o'clock (midnight) Stypes got up and remarked how " bright and beautiful " the night was (being a moonlight night), and looking down, he said, " Boys, I have slept in the middle all winter, and am very much cramped up. One of you sleep in the middle and let me take the outside, where I can stretch out." Davis got in the middle, Stypes lay down, with his left hand folded the blanket back on Davis, straightened himself out, gasped for breath three or four times, and expired ; actually starved to death

We could not take out the body and report the death until the next day, but slept as comfortably as was possible on the same blanket with our dead comrade until morning, when all above seemed "bright and beautiful," let us hope, he saw the light breaking from the other shore.

The next morning Joe Waters, P A. Davis, and the writer, of the Rangers, and three members of the 3d Vermont Infantry, carried Stypes out in a blanket, giving name, company and regiment, and piled him up with about 200 others waiting burial   The dead would often lie a week, or ten days, before burial.   The weather was very cold, and the bodies would freeze stiff in a few minutes

Wood was issued to the prisoners for fuel but three times during winter, three sticks to ten men.

There was an excuse of a hospital on the Island, where patients were taken for treatment, although when one entered its portals it was practically bidding adieu to all earthly hope   While it is true the supply of medicine in the Confederate domains was somewhat limited, yet there seemed to be ample to save life, if properly administered   Every one of the Rangers who was taken to the hospital on the Island died, with the single exception of George Nogle.   Presley A. Davis was taken there in January 1864, and died in a few days.   Thomas Dixon was taken there the last of January, 1864, and died February 6, 1864.   Jeff. McCutcheon was shot by the rebel guard for being outside of the dead line.   He was taken to the hospital and died from his wound, March 7, 1864. A. C. Hawk was taken to the hospital and died March 31, 1864.   Henry Stewart was taken to Danville, Va., with other prisoners, and died January, 25, 1864.

March 1, J. A. Cox, Richard Virts, Joseph Magaha, James Dailey, and Henry Hoover were taken to Andersonville, Ga , where all of them died.

Joseph Magaha died April 5, 1864.

Richard Virts died May 23, 1864.

James Dailey died June 17, 1864.

Henry Hoover died June 30, 1864.

J. A. Cox died July 14, 1864.

A great many prisoners were sent to the Island about the 15th of January, 1864. Very few of them were provided with shelter. They would walk to keep warm, until entirely exhausted, and all lie down in a huddle on the sand to keep from freezing. Every morning quite a number would be carried out to the dead lot, having perished during the night.

While the suffering was so intense and the mortality so great, the prison authorities would tell us of stupendous Confederate victories, point out the Confederate flag, that was displayed everywhere, as the flag that would soon wave over this entire country, and then give us a very kind invitation to take the oath of allegiance to the Confederate Government and enlist in its army, and have plenty to eat and be liberated. The plenty to eat part was tempting to the starving prisoners

Out of the 11,000 prisoners confined on the Island less than fifty availed themselves of this invitation. Be it said to the credit of the Rangers that every one of them spurned this invitation, and was emphatic in his determination to stand by the flag of his country, even if it cost him his life in a Southern prison

Men who would offer life upon the battle field for their country gave way under the weight of helpless imprisonment, brutal treatment, cold, filth and starvation. Many were reduced to the border of imbecility and delirium Is it strange that the instinct of self-

preservation should overmaster stern duty? We pity
and almost excuse the shipwrecked mariner, who,
crazed by thirst and hunger, slays and drinks the blood
of his weaker brother In a like gracious spirit, let
there be charity and forgivenness for those who stopped
short of heroic martyrdom in the hour of sore trial.
The very fact that of the men who had stood by the
Flag with such fidelity and courage, even so small a
number consented to live at such a sacrifice, is the
most melancholy proof that could be offered of the
horrible suffering which they endured.   Over five thousand, faithful unto death, sank down beneath the filth
and ruin of that horrible pit.

The few that clung to this delusion of a shadow of a
hope by swearing allegiance to the Confederacy did so
to get out of prison, and deserted at the first opportunity
and went into the Federal lines.

The prisoners were allowed to write home provided
the letters did not give information concerning the
rebels.   All letters were deposited in a box, unsealed,
and examined before they were permitted to start on
their mission northward.   Probably not more than one
letter out of a hundred was ever permitted to go.

It was impossible to resist the suffering from hunger
One of the many revolting acts of starving humanity
will be related, while others are too horrible to appear in
print.

The latter part of January, Lieut. Haight, with his
customary pomp and display, entered the prison on an
inspecting tour, accompanied by his dog   The prisoners had longed for an opportunity to waylay this canine,
and now the coveted hour had arrived.   As Haight made
his exit from the stockade, he missed his dog ; he called
long and loud but his boon companion did not show up.
Not even a bark was heard.   Haight grew furious and
threatened the prisoners with total annihilation if his

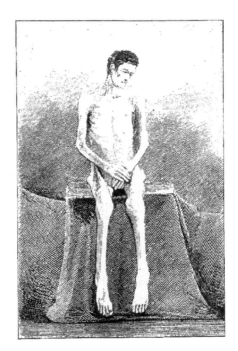

JACKSON O. BRASHEARS, 65 Ind. Mt. Inf., fellow prisoner
of the Rangers on Belle Island.

dog was not produced Every man was marched out
and searched. The process consumed an entire day.
This investigation did not reveal even the " hairs on
the dog's back " which are said to be very numerous

Haight knew the fate of his "purp" but wanted to
find and punish the guilty parties.

The truth is, some of the ravenous prisoners killed
the dog and parceled out the meat to their chums, and
he was eaten up before the search began.

Haight got partial revenge by refusing the prisoners
any rations for twenty-four hours. He never ventured
in the stockade again with a dog.

The prisoners were divided into squads of 100 each, to
facilitate the issuing of rations, etc. After January 31,
1864, 100 prisoners would be taken out every morning
and sent to Andersonville, Ga , although the prisoners
did not know that was their destination, they supposing
they were going to be exchanged, and sent North

Every morning, when a squad would be called for,
Lieut. Haight would call the captain of the squad to
identify his own men. He and Haight would take their
position on the parapet beside the gate, and when any
attempted to go out that did not belong to that hundred
the captain would point them out to Haight, when
down would come his big club and knock them back to
starve a little more

The Rangers naturally put considerable stress on liberty, and willingly assumed the risk of running the
gauntlet in order that they might get out before the
squad they belonged to was called.

On one occasion the writer endeavored to get out by
passing himself off as belonging to the squad that was
passing out, and had almost succeeded, when he was de-
tected. Haight brought down his big club and knocked
him into the dead-line ditch, that contained about eight
inches of water with thin ice over it. He fell in this water,

and without any fire to dry his clothes, with the mercury about zero, he almost froze ; he lay for one week apparently at death's door, but finally rallied sufficiently to leave the Island with his squad, Monday, March 21, 1864   We were so weak that it took an hour and a half to march from Belle Isle to Richmond, three-fourths of a mile.   Our squad, like others that preceded us, was doomed for Andersonville.   We were to leave Richmond March 22 for that place.

During the night of the 21st a dispatch was received from City Point, " Send one hundred Yankee prisoners to be exchanged for one hundred Confederate prisoners just arrived from the North "

> " And why should you fear that the future
> Has such disappointments in store ?
> Perchance the hand which guides us
> Will open some other door "

Our squad being ready for immediate shipment, the orders for Andersonville were revoked, and we were ordered to march to the boat early Tuesday morning, March 22, 1864, to embark for City Point

The news was first broken to the prisoners a few minutes before the time of departure, and created unbounded enthusiasm.   Some cheered, while others sang patriotic airs.   As we had received similar news on several occasions, all did not accept it ; finally the doors swung open, and we were ordered to march out, and as we did so the rebels gave each prisoner a small corn pone, about as large as the bottom of a small tin cup and one inch thick.   As we came in sight of the boat that was to carry us down the river the boys gave their corn pones a toss down the hill into the James

When all had been safely packed on the little steamboat, William Allison, Joseph Waters, the writer, and several others crowded into the engine room in their eagerness to get warm.   What a delightful transition, to get thawed out after being frozen all winter.   But, like most good things, it came at a sacrifice, as the thawing-out process made us very sick.   We were put out on deck, much to our relief, where we soon froze up again.   At 4 o'clock in the evening, we came in view of our steamboat, "City of New York," and the first object sighted was the American Flag, the Stars and Stripes. We wish we could convey to the reader the beauties of that dear old Flag as it appeared to the prisoners.   Those physically able cheered the dear old emblem of liberty, a grand privilege that had been denied them for nearly seven months.   Others tried their best to yell, but were so overcome with joy that they could not speak, but wept like little children ; it floated majestically from the mast of the steamer, bidding defiance to its foes, it seemingly said, " Come, all ye oppressed of every clime, beneath my folds, and you shall be forever free."

" Now it catches the gleam of the morning's first beam,
In full glory reflected, now shines on the stream !—
'Tis the STAR SPANGLED BANNER, oh, long may it wave
O'er the land of the free, and the home of the brave "

The Rangers included in this exchange were James H. Beatty, Joseph Waters, W H Angelow, George Nogle, George Swope, and the writer.

The strong and vigorous constitutions of Beatty and Waters enabled them, to some extent, to better resist the hardships of prison life than others, and, while both were greatly reduced in flesh, they gained rapidly and joined the command in April, 1864.

Angelow and Nogle were both sick, and were sent to the hospital at Annapolis, Md., remaining for two months, returning to the company in May

George Swope died, a few days after his arrival at Annapolis, from the effects of prison exposure.

The writer was a physical wreck from prison life, as both feet were badly frozen, and, having partially lost the use of one side, he was confined in the hospital at Annapolis, Md., for four months, returning to the company in July, although it was over one year before he recovered.

Jackson O Brashear, Company D, 65th Indiana Infantry, whose picture is to be found in this book, was a prisoner on Belle Isle, and belonged to the same squad with the Rangers, exchanged at the same time, and was a patient in the hospital at Annapolis, Md., with them. The photograph was taken two weeks after he was exchanged, and published in *Frank Leslie's Weekly*, June 18, 1864, and also printed in the Report of the United States Sanitary Commission in the summer of 1864. His emaciated condition is a fair average of the returned prisoners from Belle Isle and Andersonville He is now a successful farmer in Indiana

. Of those of the Rangers taken prisoner near Waterford, May 17 1864—James H Beatty, William Bull, Peter Dorherty, John Ambrose, and H. C. Fouch—James H Beatty made his escape the day of capture, while Ambrose, Dorherty, Bull, and Fouch were taken to Richmond. Ambrose was exchanged in five months. Bull, Dorherty, and Fouch were taken to Andersonville, Ga , where Fouch died September 18, 1864 Bull and Dorherty remained there until, after the surrender of Gen. Lee, when the Confederates hastened to release the Union prisoners.

A train load of nearly 800 was started for Vicksburg, Miss , with two of the Rangers, Bull and Dorherty, on board. When about 200 miles from Andersonville, by some unknown cause, there was a disastrous railroad accident, resulting in the killing and wounding of nearly all on board. Peter Dorherty was killed. Bull was badly bruised, but was taken on to Vicksburg, where he, with over 2,000 paroled prisoners, were placed on board the steamboat " Sultana," and started up the river for Cincinnati.

At Memphis the boat unloaded a quantity of freight and took on a supply of coal and continued the journey Six miles above Memphis, April 27, soon after midnight, her boilers exploded with terrific force, and the vessel was burned to the water's edge and sank   There were 1,443 of the paroled prisoners scalded, blown up, or drowned, at once.   Of those rescued 300 soon died of scalds and exposure, making the total loss of prisoners over 1,750.   Of 27 lady passengers only one was saved

William Bull, the only one of the Rangers on board, was blown the Lord only knows where   He was picked up the next morning about nine miles below the scene of the disaster, near the Arkansas shore ; he had crawled on a piece of board, a fragment of the vessel, and was endeavoring to reach the shore.   He was in the water five hours when rescued, and was taken to the hospital in Memphis, Tenn , where by kind and devoted attention by the ladies of the United States Christian Commission he was nursed back to life   When able to travel he was sent to Camp Chase, Columbus, Ohio, and mustered out.   On his arrival at Harpers Ferry he found the war over, the Rangers mustered out and busily engaged endeavoring to build up the waste places made desolate by the ravages of war.

No one knew the exact cause of the disaster.   It was charged that Charles Dale, a Confederate blockade runner, placed a torpedo in a lump of coal and laid it on top of the pile, while the vessel was taking coal at Memphis.

William Streeter, of St. Louis, Mo , claims Dale told him he did it on purpose to destroy the vessel

Of those taken prisoners October 14, 1864, at Adamstown, Md., John Coates died in prison, and is numbered among the unknown in the National Cemetery at Rich-

mond   In February, 1865, Sergt. John W. Forsythe
and Dan Burnett, Company B, and Sergt. J. N Johnson, of Company A, were exchanged

Sergt , now Rev., John W Forsythe, of Lu Verne,
Iowa, has published an exceedingly interesting pamph-
let of 50 pages, entitled, "Guerrilla Warfare, and Life
in Libby," in which he gives a thrilling account of
some of the perilous experiences of the Rangers, together with a minute and reliable account of the priva-
tions and hardships of those taken prisoners at Adamstown and confined in Libby Prison.   His story is
founded on personal experience, and is worthy of
perusal

Of those taken prisoners November 28 at Goresville,
Peter Fry died January 27, 1865.   The records show
him to be buried in the National Cemetery at Richmond, in grave No 1091

The same records show him to have died in prison
at Salisbury, North Carolina, and to be buried in the
National Cemetery, at the latter place, in grave No 1164.
The date, name, company and regiment is the same in
both places, the only difference being in number of the
grave.   Of course it is impossible to state in which place
he is buried.   The error probably occurred in keeping
the record, or in getting it printed.

The others that were taken prisoner with him were
exchanged in February, 1865.

Those taken prisoners at Keyes Switch, April 6,
1865, were released in a few days.

In Conclusion.

The unparalleled severities of a four years' campaign
have told upon the constitutional strength even of the
fortunate soldier who marched to the music of the
Union, and slept only beneath the folds of the Flag for
which he fought ; but they whom fickle fortune cast in

Southern prisons, where they lay for long dreary months, when gaunt famine stalked by noonday, and pestilence walked by night, returned—if they returned at all—but wrecks of their former selves Wherever stretched the form of a Union prisoner, there rose the signal for cruelty and the cry of agony, and there, day by day, grew the skeleton graves of the nameless dead ; but braving and enduring all this, some thousands have returned to you. You will bear with me, and these noble men will pardon me, while, in conclusion, I speak one word for them. The survivors of a rebel prison pen, though few, have endured and suffered what you never can, and I hope your children never may. With less strength, and more of sad and bitter memories, he is with you, and whether he asks it or not, will deserve at your hands no ordinary share of kindly consideration. If he asks leave to toil, give it him before it be too late ; if he needs kindness and encouragement, bestow them freely while you may ; if he seeks charity at your hands, remember that "the poor you have always with you," but him you have not always, and withhold it not.

If you find him making organized effort to provide for the widow and the orphan, remember that it grows out of the heart-sympathy which clusters around the memories of the comrade who perished by his side.

Finally, permit me to commend to the grateful consideration of the noble, generous people, alike the sol- dier who has given his strength, however small ; the prisoner who sacrificed his health ; the widow who has offered up her husband , the mother whose heart bleeds for her only boy ; the orphan who knows only that its father went out to battle and comes no more forever ; and the lonely, distant grave of the martyr who sleeps alone in a strange soil, that liberty, freedom, and peace might come to ours and our children's children forever.

ROSTER OF COMPANY A.

No	Rank	Names	Mustered in—		Remarks
			Date	Place.	
1	Captain..	Samuel C. Means ...	June 20, 1862	Harpers Ferry...	Resigned on account of wounds.
2	Do	Daniel M. Keyes ..	. do .	Lovettsville	Resigned on account of wounds
3	1st Lieut..	Luther W Slater .	...do	..... do	
4	Do	Edwin R. Gover ...	.....do ..	. do	Wounded near Fairfax C. H., Dec., 1864, discharged on account of wounds.
5	2d Lieut ..	Robert Graham......	.....do ..	Waterford	
6	{ Drill } { Master }	Chas. A Webster ...	.. do .	Valley Church ..	Hung at Richmond, Va., by the rebels, April 10, 1863.
7	1st Sergt...	Jas A. Cox	... do	Lovettsville .	Wounded at Waterford, Aug. 27, 1862, died at Andersonville, July 14, 1864.
8	Q M S.	Chas F Anderson	.....do	..... do	Killed at Harpers Ferry, Nov 1, 1863
9	Do......	Edward T White .	.... do	..... do	

R—15

10	C. S......	Milton S. Gregg......	June 20, 1862	Lovettsville......	Killed near Lovettsville, Va., March 1863.
11	1st Sergt...	Jas. H. Corbin......	...do......	...do......	
12	Do......	Joseph T. Divine......	...do......	Waterford......	Wounded at Charlestown, Va., Oct. 18, 1863; killed at Taylorstown, Va., Dec. 24, 1864.
13	Do......	F. B. Anderson......	...do......	Lovettsville......	
14	2d Sergt...	D. E. B. Hough......	...do......	do......	Wounded at Waterford Aug. 27, 1862, and Neersville, Va., Sept. 30, 1863
15	3d Sergt...	Jas. W. Gregg......	...do......	do......	
16	4th Sergt...	John P. Hickman......	...do......	do......	Wounded at Charlestown, Va., Oct. 18, 1863.
17	5th Sergt...	James H. Beatty......	...do......	do......	
18	6th Sergt...	J. N. Johnson......	...do......	Point of Rocks...	Wounded at Keys Switch, April 6, 1865; wounded, Waterford, Aug. 27, 1862; Adamstown, Md., Oct. 14, 1864.
19	Corporal...	Robert W. Hough...	...do......	Waterford......	
20	Do......	Henry C. Hough......	...do......	do......	Wounded at Charlestown, Va., Oct. 18, 1863.
21	Do......	Daniel J. Harper......	...do......	do......	
22	Do......	T. J. McCutcheon......	...do......	do......	Died from wounds at Richmond, Va., Mar. 7, 1864.
23	Do......	George V. Kern......	Nov. 1, 1863	Harpers Ferry...	

24	Corporal...	Jacob Cordell	June 20, 1862	Lovettsville	Wounded at Leesburg, Sept. 2, 1862, and at Goresville, Va , Nov 28, 1864.
25	Do......	George H. Harper...	Aug. 24, 1862	Waterford	Wounded at Waterford, Va., Aug 27, 1862
26	Do......	Samuel E. Tritapoe.	July 23, 1862	Lovettsville	
27	Do......	T W Franklin .	July 1, 1862	. do	
28	Do......	Samuel C. Hough .	June 20, 1862	.... do	
29	Bugler. ...	John S Densmore...	.. do	.... do	
30	Privates ...	Agan, Thomas W...	Feb. 12, 1863	Berlin, Md .	
31	Do....	Ambrose, John	Mch 1, 1863	.... do	
32	Do	Angelow, W. H	June 20, 1862	Lovettsville	
33	Do	Armstrong, John .	....	....	
34	Do ...	Atwell, C. M	June 20, 1862	Waterford	Transferred to Company B.
35	Do .	Bagent, Joseph.	April 2, 1863	Berlin, Md......	Wounded at Adamstown, Md., Oct 14, 1864
36	Do	Best, M. H	June 20, 1862	Lovettsville ...	Wounded at Leesburg Sept 2, 1862; died in prison, Richmond
37	Do.....	Baker, Charles.......	....do	.. ... do	
38	Do	Baker, George W ...	....do	... do	Wounded at Leesburg, Sept. 2, 1862.
39	Do ...	Bull, William	Mch. 1, 1863	Berlin, Md. ..	
40	Do ...	Bond, Edward........	....do	.... do	Died at Point of Rocks, Md., Feb. 5, 1864.
41	Do ..	Boryer, Jacob E ..	June 20, 1862	Lovettsville	Discharged on account of wounds received Sept 2, 1862, at Leesburg.

No.	Rank	Name	Date	Residence	Remarks
42	Privates	Cantwell, J T	June 20 1862	Lovettsville	Discharged on account of disability
43	Do	Coates, John	Feb 10, 1864	Pot. Furnace	Died in rebel prison.
44	Do	Cooper, W. J	June 20, 1862	Lovettsville	
45	Do	Cooper, S. J	do	do	
46	Do	Curry, Charles E.	Dec 21, 1863	Point of Rocks	Transferred to Company B.
47	Do	Dugan, Henry	Aug. 15, 1862	do	Died in rebel prison, Andersonville, Ga., June 17, 1864
48	Do	Daily, James	Oct. 25, 1862	do	
49	Do	Davis, George P.	Mch. 3, 1863	Berlin, Md	Died in rebel prison, Richmond, Va.
50	Do	Davis, Presley A.	do	do	
51	Do	Davis, John M	June 20, 1862	Lovettsville	Died in rebel prison, Richmond, Va., Feb. 5, 1864.
52	Do	Dixon, Thomas			Killed at Waterford, Va., Aug. 27, 1862.
53	Do	Dixon, Charles	do	do	Killed at Waterford, Va , Aug. 27, 1862.
54	Do	Dixon, Henry	do	do	Transferred to Company B
55	Do	Dixon, Jacob	Sept. 1, 1862	Waterford	Killed in Alabama, 1865.
56	Do	Dorherty, Peter	Mch. 1, 1863	Berlin, Md	
57	Do	Divine, George	June 20, 1862	Lovettsville	Discharged on account of wounds, Leesburg, Sept. 2, 1862
58	Do	Everhart, Armistead	do	do	
59	Do	Fry, Samuel	do	do	

No.	Rank	Name	Enrolled	Place	Remarks
60	Privates	Fry, Joseph	June 20, 1862	Lovettsville	Wounded at Goresville, Nov 28, 1864, died in rebel prison, Richmond, Jan 27, 1865.
61	Do	Fry, Peter C	Jan. 2, 1863	Point of Rocks	
62	Do	Fouch, Temple	June 20, 1862	Lovettsville	Died in rebel prison, Andersonville, Ga, Sept 18, 1864.
63	Do	Fouch, H. C	...do...	......do...	
64	Do	Fouch, Thomas	July 27, 1863	Point of Rocks	Wounded at Point of Rocks, Md.
65	Do	Forsythe, J. W	June 20, 1862	Lovettsville	Transferred to Company B
66	Do	Goodhart, Briscoe	Aug. 22, 1862	Waterford	Wounded, leg broken at Berryville, Va, April, 1863.
67	Do	Hough, William	June 20, 1862	Lovettsville	
68	Do	Hough, Joseph F	......do...	......do...	
69	Do	Hough, George W	......do...	......do...	Died at Berlin, Md, 1863
70	Do	Hough, Isaac S	....	....	Wounded at Middletown, Md., July 7, 1864
71	Do	Hawk, A. C	Nov. 17, 1862	Point of Rocks	Died in rebel prison, Richmond, March 31, 1864.
72	Do	Heater, P. H	Jan. 27, 1863	......do...	
73	Do	Hoover, H. W	Mch. 1, 1863	Berlin, Md	
74	Do	Harper, R S	June 20, 1862	Waterford	Died in rebel prison, Andersonville, Ga, June 30-1864.

75	Privates	Hardy, W H	Dec 21, 1863	Point of Rocks	Discharged on account of wounds received at Waterford, Aug. 27, 1862.
76	Do	Jacobs, Edward N.	June 20, 1862	Lovettsville	
77	Do	Keyes, W S	Nov. 1, 1862	do	Wounded at Leesburg, Va., Sept. 2, 1862
78	Do	Long, Jacob	July 15, 1862	do	
79	Do	Lenhart, J. W.	Feb 3, 1863	Point of Rocks	Wounded at Goresville, collar bone broken, Nov. 28, 1864.
80	Do	Magaha, Joseph	June 20, 1862	Lovettsville	Died in rebel prison, Andersonville Ga, April 5, 1864.
81	Do	Miles, Peter	June 20, 1862	Lovettsville	Died in rebel prison, Castle Thunder, Richmond.
82	Do	Morman, Frank	do	do	Killed at Leesburg, Va , Sept. 2, 1862.
83	Do	Monegan, James	Dec. 8, 1862	Point of Rocks	Killed at Waterford, Vd , May 17, 1864.
84	Do	Moreland, C F	Feb 24, 1864	do	
85	Do	Myers, J. R	do	do	
86	Do	Mullen, Michael	June 20, 1862	Lovettsville	Wounded at Waterford Dec., 1862, died at Annapolis, Md., 1863.
87	Do	Mock, Albert C	July 25, 1863	Point of Rocks	
88	Do	McDade, Charles	June 20, 1862	Lovettsville	

No.	Rank	Name	Date	Place	Remarks
89	Privates ..	McDevitt, John	Jan. 25, 1863	Point of Rocks .	Wounded at Charlestown, Oct 18, 1863.
90	Do	Nogle, W George.	July 15, 1862	Waterford	Died in rebel prison, Richmond, Va.
91	Do	Pekam, Charles. ..	Jan. 25, 1863	Point of Rocks ..	Transferred to Company B.
92	Do ...	Paxton, F D..			
93	Do.....	Rinker, F. P	June 20, 1862	Lovettsville	Wounded at Lovettsville; died in rebel prison, Andersonville, May, 8, 1864.
94	Do....	Rinker, Charles E.	Feb 24, 1864	Point of Rocks...	Killed at Waterford May 17, 1864
95	Do......	Ritchie, Joseph T.	June 20, 1862	Lovettsville	
96	Do	Ryan, Michael	Mch. 8, 1863	Berlin, Md .	
97	Do .	Stoneburner, James	June 20, 1862	Lovettsville	Died in rebel prison
98	Do......	Stewart, H	Aug 29, 1863	Berlin, Md. .	Died in rebel prison, Danville, Va , Jan 25, 1864
99	Do.	Swope, George	Oct 12, 1863	Harpers Ferry...	Died at Annapolis, Md.
100	Do...	Shores, George W	Aug 20, 1863	Berlin	
101	Do ...	Snoots, Charles H	June 20, 1862	Lovettsville	
102	Do ...	Spring, Charles L	...do	do	
103	Do....	Shakelford, J W .	.... do	do	Died at small pox hospital Weverton, Md.
104	Do	Shakelford, S	..do	. do	Wounded at Leesburg, Sept. 2, 1862 ; died in rebel prison, Andersonville, Ga , May 7, 1864.

No.	Rank	Name	Date	Place	Remarks
105	Privates	Stout, Charles E	June 20, 1862	Lovettsville	Died at small pox hospital, Weverton, Md.
106	Do	Shoemaker, Wm	....do........	.... do	Died in rebel prison, Castle Thunder, Richmond, Va.
107	Do	Snyder, Edward	Mch. 14, 1863	Berlin, Md	
108	Do	Tritapoe, George C.	June 24, 1863	Relay House	
109	Do	Taylor, John	June 3, 1863	Berlin, Md	
110	Do	Thomas, Notly W	Aug. 1, 1863	.... do	
111	Do	Virts, John W	Jan. 1863	Waterford	Wounded at Point of Rocks, June 17, 1863.
112	Do	Virts, Charles W	Feb. 24, 1864	Point of Rocks	
113	Do	Virts, R. A	Mch. 3, 1863	Berryville	Died in rebel prison, Andersonville, Ga., May 23, 1864.
114	Do	White, C. W	June 20, 1862	Lovettsville	
115	Do	Waters, Joseph	......do	Lovettsville	Wounded at the Valley Church, July, 1862; wounded at Adamstown, Md.
116	Do	Waters, George H	Oct. 29, 1863	Harpers Ferry	Killed at Licksville, Md., Oct. 14, 1864.
117	Do	Wright, James T	June 20, 1862	Lovettsville	
118	Do	Welsh, George	....do ..	.... do	
119	Do	Wilt, George	Mch. 31, 1863	Berryville	
120	Do	Zee, Robert	Dec. 1, 1862	Waterford	

Total enlistments Company A 120 ; total loss 44.

Comparative Losses.

	Per cent.		Per cent
Rangers	0 36	10th New York Cavalry	0.17
1st Maine Cavalry	0.18	8th Indiana Cavalry	0.21
1st Vermont Cavalry	0 20	1st Michigan Cavalry	0.16
2d New York Cavalry	0.14	5th Michigan Cavalry	0.23
8th New York Cavalry	0.15	6th Michigan Cavalry	0.24
1st New Jersey Cavalry	0.15		

Having been unsuccessful in getting a copy of the muster roll of Company B from the War Department, the present roll is reproduced from memory, and there may be omissions.

Captain—
  James W. Grubb.*
First Lieutenant—
  Charles M. Atwell.*
Second Lieutenant—
  Augustus C. Rhodes.
First Sergeant—
  George H. Hickman.
Sergeants—
  Fenton D Paxton.
  John W. Forsythe.
  Thomas Dewire.
  Charles Stewart.
Corporals—
  John Chamblin
  Randolph Nichols.*
  Hiram Latham.
  Noble Dean
  Phillip Pritchard.*
  Thomas Coates.*
Privates—
  George Allen.
  Jacob Ailen.
  J. C. Ayton.
  James Ault.
  John Aikison
  Abraham Atkins.
  G. W. Bachus.
  George Ball.
  G W. Bentz
  Edward Butt
  Daniel Burnett
  J F. Cantwell
  John Cason.
  John Canall
  C. Creswell.
  Henry Cole.

Edward Dean.
Jacob Dixon.
Thomas Dixon *
John Dillon
James Delaney.
Henry Dugan.
James Foreman.
William Forsythe.
W J. Gore.
J. W Harrison.
Thomas Harrison.
James W Hawk.
John W. Hawk *
William Harduat.
Henry Haines.*
John Kidwell.*
Mark Kiverler.
Benjamin Matthews.
William Marby.
George Monday
Thomas Morrisey.
John Mock.
James McKinney.*
Franklin Null.
William Nunberger.
John Orrison.
Harry Peters.
Charles Rice.
N B. Riley
G. W Rippeon.
Ewell Rose
Joseph Ryton.
John Scarlett.
John Sponceller.
Mathias Spong.
R. H Wallace.
James Wilson.

* Dead

CPSIA information can be obtained
at www.ICGtesting.com
Printed in the USA
BVHW060614050222
627862BV00003B/44

9 781298 562333